To Marisa, who gave me the inspiration to write this;
to Valeria, who helped me choose the right path;
and to all those who help people find fulfillment in their lives.

Contents

Preface

Human happiness. Where does it come from, what might contribute to or improve it, how can we aspire to more of it?

Some of the vast and still-growing literature on this topic is based on spiritual insights or belief systems. Ongoing empirical research is funded by the National Institutes of Health (NIH) and based on the findings of research psychologists and other social scientists. Yet even more information on happiness is simply practical, based on the life experiences and personal observations of individual authors.

This book, *Fulfilled!*, offers a way of thinking about life's opportunities and challenges that is different in important ways from all of these sources. Not contradictory, but different—complementary, if you will. The insights and methods proposed here are immediately actionable by any reader at any stage of life. It seems to me and my colleagues at the Metrus Group that these may be of particular interest to millennials—individuals in the early stages of their careers and lives. And yet, having said that, we find forty-, fifty-, and sixty-somethings (even septo- and octogenarians) wrestling with what they want to do with the rest of their lives!

Fulfilled! has a strong foundation in field research and professional practice, but it is the research and practice not of an academic psychologist or a practicing therapist but of an organizational psychologist who has spent twenty-five years as a research and management consultant in organizations of all walks of life—startups, not-for-profits, Fortune 500s, government, and even church groups. As the founder and principal of Metrus Group, Inc., I and my colleagues have studied hundreds of companies and interviewed and surveyed tens of thousands of people, ranging from the C-suite executives to the customer service reps, union shop floor employees, and service delivery personnel. We have studied installers, sales reps, clerks, scientists, engineers, HR managers, accountants, systems designers, production employees, retail staff, lawyers, and mill workers.

We have published our findings in a series of books readily available to academics and lay audiences as well. But this book is a summary of our findings intended not for my academic colleagues but for practical application by readers like you.

Reflections on this body of work led us to the concept of *fulfillment* as a critical quality that is evident when individuals are conscientiously living in accordance with a plan that brings out the best in themselves. They feel fulfilled when they are living and working in alignment with their values and those of their friends, family, colleagues, and employers; utilizing skills and interests both on and off the job that represent their highest capabilities; and fully engaged in the significance and purpose of their work, family, and life overall.

Given the way technology, especially social media, and the fluid nature of modern lives and roles are intermixing through a 24-7 workweek, the importance of this elusive but urgent goal of fulfillment may well be felt most deeply by millennials.

The old concept of work-life balance applies here, but as a term, it is almost too weak to describe the full interpenetration of work life and personal life, career and relationships, play and travel that characterizes many working people today at all stages of their careers—but perhaps most especially those members of the younger generation who are most heavily invested in the new and social media. These new technologies of communication have all but dissolved traditional distinctions of home and office, work time and personal time, career and life.

Fulfillment has two important faces, and they both must be considered. One is a quality of life and work now: Is the way I spend my day, my week, fulfilling? The other is a culmination—a retrospective assessment of one's life as a whole—toward the end of a career, perhaps as one generation begins to relinquish control to its successors. Obviously, this aspect turns out to be of greatest interest to my fellow baby boomers.

Has my life been fulfilling? Can I claim a sense of fulfillment overall as I take stock, look back, make a holistic sounding of the world and whatever mark I have been able to leave on it? How, in other words, does one achieve the full sense of *fulfillment*? Happiness as we have come to understand it is certainly one part of fulfillment, to be sure—at least a reasonable modicum of personal and career success, yes. Some minimum denominator of good health is not to be denied.

But what concerns us most, and what inspired this book, are those factors all of us can control and those decisions all of us must make—or fail to consciously make—that lead to either rich rewards or wasted opportunities, rewarding or neglected friendships, fruitful or sterile marriages, soul-deadening work or a sense of "flow," vegging out or passionately re-creating our energies and enthusiasms in our off hours. Career counseling may well be helpful for persons seeking personal fulfillment. So may traditional forms of therapy. Both are important, even critical at times, but neither captures the full dimensions of fulfillment we discuss in this book.

In recent years, we at the Metrus Institute have perceived a major unmet need, and potential application, for frameworks such as People Equity and balanced or strategic scorecarding approaches—which are often employed in business—to be used by individuals. The same techniques that companies have used for years now to better understand, align, and energize their workforces can be turned around for the benefit of both the organization and the individual. They can and should be used by the individuals in those same workforces to better understand and align their own lives. The telescope that has served corporate America by looking outward can also produce powerful insights as a microscope looking inward.

That is what this book is about. In recent years, we have supplemented our work as management consultants with open-ended interviews and surveys of hundreds of individuals across generations, roles, relationships, and geographies. From all of this, we have found an incredible interest in better understanding, anticipating, and making use of those everyday actions and decisions—in this book, we call them *drivers*—that can enable anyone to live his or her life with greater purpose, more focus, and more conscious enjoyment.

To understand fully what is entailed by that engaging prospect, and how anyone can use and profit from these simple but powerful tools—at any age—we invite you to explore and ultimately live a life of fulfillment.

William A. Schiemann
July 14, 2016

INTRODUCTION

Learning from Those Who Have Created Rich and Rewarding Lives

Marisa is a marathoner, mother of three, consummate devotee of theater and music, and a former client of mine. She could be someone you work with daily in your organization. She works hard. She joined her company because she wanted to make a difference in addition to making a living. She did the normal things that people do in companies—she went to meetings, completed reports, and finished her assignments.

When I spent a little more time with her, I realized she had something special going on. She was tireless in her efforts to bring about change, digging in to help her employer transform its business. She generated new ideas, figured out ways to overcome historical blocks, coached leaders, and revved the team. Culturally, this organization was tired, but she brought it new energy. She rallied support for new thinking and processes that my firm introduced to them, and by doing so, her company was transformed into a powerhouse that began to dominate its industry. She was one of the most upbeat, optimistic people I have ever known. While being optimistic is nice, it was her tenacity to help the team reach goals that set her apart. When others said "can't," she said, "why not?"

Not only was Marisa an inspiring leader in her company; she had a full life outside of work that included running, helping her children grow, and participating in community and professional groups. She was contagiously vivacious. She spoke at professional conferences, inspiring younger people to become all they could be. However, nothing had been handed to her on a silver platter. The Marisa I met had recovered from a difficult, flawed first marriage, requiring her to raise two children with limited resources. When her marriage dissolved, she didn't even know what type of work she could do. She was the quintessential bootstrapper, going to employers and saying, "I can do that."

Despite no business education or experience, she landed one job as an HR trainee and followed that with a promotion to a project manager in training and development. When her company needed someone in a new role, she once again raised her hand and said, "I can do that." She had to work long hours to figure out what she had just committed herself to do. She also worked hard on finding and creating relationships with experts who knew far more than she knew but who felt flattered to be her mentor and teacher. When I met her, she had scaled the corporate walls to the position of vice president. If you had clicked back ten years, you would not have thought it possible. Was it chance? Not on your life! Perseverance, a great attitude, moxie, and a little bit of luck got her to where she was.

In addition to everything else, she was caring for a daughter who had serious medical challenges and dealing with other family traumas. But the real bombshell dropped in a quiet conversation at The Conference Board in New York. After our session finished, she informed me that she had just been diagnosed with stage-four pancreatic cancer. Doctors were giving her only six to nine months to live. I was devastated, almost unable to speak, with tears welling up in my eyes. Remarkably, she maintained a radiant glow of hopefulness—more than I could possibly muster at that moment. She looked me in the eyes and said, "I will beat this!" While I knew Marisa well, I have to confess I had my doubts. After all, her hospital is known for its reputation in cancer diagnosis and treatment, and they didn't give her much of a chance. I knew she was a miracle worker, but no one is indestructible.

As iconic radio broadcaster Paul Harvey used to say, "And now, for the rest of the story." I am delighted to report that the end of this story is a happy one for Marisa and everyone she touched. Among the cohort of pancreatic cancer patients who have been given this dreadful diagnosis, she is among the scarce few to have survived for more than ten years—and is still going.

I sat down with Marisa recently and asked her how she did it. She shocked me with her answer. She said, "I applied what you taught us at work to my own life. I used the scorecarding and alignment approaches that you had taught my company."

I'm sure I had a blank stare because this simply did not compute for me, so I asked her to elaborate. She went on to explain how she quickly sat down and set clear goals for her life. Of course, the big, audacious goal was to beat cancer and go on living. But the first goal was to live—for one year. Then she listed all the things she had to do, her drivers of life, to give herself a chance. She had to shed work for the time being and find an oncologist who believed she could do it—no small feat, as she described the tedious process of searching to find one. Most important, she had to end relationships with the people in her life who were not on her "survival team." She told one relative that she would not be able to see her again if she could not get on the "positive team."

Marisa then set out to learn from survivors and establish measures for herself for many different drivers of survival: weight, energy, stomach pain, diet, spirit, exercise, and medical indicators. She sought out the best advice in each of these areas. She studied and found spiritual healers, sought alternative medical advice, discovered different dietary approaches, tried experimental medicine, and found workable exercise routines. Her "dream team" of advisors grew, and her indicators gave her hope as she worked her plan unrelentingly. She believed that energy and optimism were critical factors and managed to keep both high despite the debilitating effects of chemotherapy and some setbacks along the way.

In the end, it worked. Her success story has been told on multiple network news shows and in major magazines, and she has now become a life mastery coach and consultant for others who are facing life challenges. On my suggestion, one former colleague who was diagnosed with cancer recently met with her and sent me a note saying it was transformative, thanking me for connecting them. He now feels he can turn his life around.

As I concluded my recent conversation with her, I felt enriched, almost giddy, and more fulfilled personally. But the real point of Marisa's story is not about beating cancer; it's about taking control of your life—at work, at home, and in your relationships and hobbies. Although Marisa talks about the incredible holism and fulfillment in her life now, it was not always so. Cancer was the trigger that caused her to rethink many aspects of her life and to examine the level of fulfillment she was experiencing. Her business success taught her that you can create a far different outcome if you work from design instead of accepting what comes your way by default.

This book is about the journey to developing a profound sense of fulfillment in your life. It is not an easy road, and it will be harder for some, but it is a road that can lead you to incredible richness in your life—a feeling that you are not only happy, but your life has made a difference to you, your family, and those you touch.

There is no such thing as a perfect ability to predict success or fulfillment, but you can stack the odds in your favor. That is exactly what Marisa did. She focused on her life goal and did everything in her power to manage her life drivers, which I will discuss in a later chapter. She was steering her life ship through shark-infested waters of naysayers. She is a role model for me—and now for many others—of how we must draw on all of our energy to achieve our dreams.

Her story, my own journey, and my experiences with so many people I have interviewed over the years provided the impetus to dig deeper into fulfillment, to conduct additional research, and to share what we have learned about life fulfillment with others. Upon reflection, just as Marisa said a decade ago after the shock of her initial diagnosis, I realized that many of the tools that we use in business can be of great help to us as individuals. There is also a substantial body of research on happiness and success that one can draw on throughout the quest for fulfillment.

However, happiness and success are not synonymous with fulfillment. Fulfillment comes from having achieved a deeper sense of purpose, one that combines the end-of-life gratification that one's life has been meaningful with the ongoing day-to-day happiness that is important along the way.

ARE *YOU* FULFILLED?

Would you say you are totally fulfilled today—feeling not only daily happiness or job satisfaction but a deeper sense of your mission in life and where you hope to end up eventually?

A majority of people we studied said no. And yet, nearly everyone I meet or interview tells me they would like to be more fulfilled. Some suggest that perhaps this is a fleeting fancy, passed along to us by our parents or early childhood books. Perhaps in a quixotic way, this is an impossible dream. But I think not. In fact, there is evidence to the contrary.

It is often reported that those in remote, undeveloped places are often more fulfilled than those in highly developed nations. Why are people happier in places like Costa Rica, for example, than in South Korea, with its much higher wealth and standard of living? Professor of psychology Ed Diener of the University of Illinois at Urbana-Champaign said that most people around the world report being relatively happy. However, few people around the world consider themselves extremely happy.[1] Why is that?

There is growing evidence that certain factors contribute to a fulfilling and satisfying life. And the good news is that we have a good deal of control over those factors. While studies vary somewhat, research has shown that we can control 40 to 60 percent of our happiness, while only a small percentage of happiness is explained by differences in life circumstances.

As researcher Sonja Lyubomirsky describes in her book *The How of Happiness*, "whether we are rich or poor, healthy or unhealthy, beautiful or plain, married or divorced" only contributes 10 percent to happiness.[2] While we cannot control where we are born or alter our genetic makeup, we can still influence our daily happiness and many factors that lead to life fulfillment.[3, 4] Before we explore the keys to fulfillment, I'll tell you a little about my path and how I got to where I am today.

MY JOURNEY

Like many high school students, I tried different classes as well as different part-time and summer jobs. In school, I pursued music and science, both of which I excelled at and liked. My jobs included being a retail clerk, a lawn mowing and landscaping worker, a drill press operator, an assembly line worker, a camera salesman, a cub reporter, and a road paver (I only lasted one day in the tar!). But each of these opportunities (I didn't see them as opportunities then) afforded me a chance to rule out certain paths in my life—ones I knew would not be fulfilling.

At the same time, each experience gave me an opportunity to think about what would fulfill me. I liked meeting people at town councils and school boards while working as a cub reporter. I enjoyed helping people design landscapes (less so the digging!) or consulting with them on the right gardening products at my hardware store job. I even found some aspects of selling intriguing. These interests set the stage for future choices.

While my grades in high school were good, I had no role models in my extended family to look to. No one had gone to college before me, and my guidance counseling in school was nonexistent. My father worked six days a week, and my mother worked full time (at a time when most moms stayed home), trying to save enough money to provide opportunities for my sister and me, but I realized that I was breaking new ground. I knew I liked music, math, and science and tossed the dice, selecting an engineering school that, it appeared, would combine the latter two.

At age nineteen, I could have used guidance when I concluded that my primary major in college was not a good fit for me and I needed to find a path forward. I knew I enjoyed being an entertainer at a radio station and the financial and political challenge of being treasurer of the student government, along with playing cards and touch football with friends, but those avocations led me to the dean's list. No, not the dean's list you may be thinking of, but academic probation. I was told I had one semester to improve my grades or I would be DJing and playing cards on the street. I spent some serious time afraid and in reflection. I did not want to fail my parents, who had worked so hard to enable me to go to college, but most importantly, I couldn't let myself down. I had always thought of myself as a winner until then.

Two things changed my life, almost by accident. I began dating my future wife, and I began working as a door-to-door pollster for a professor. I quickly found that I particularly enjoyed designing experiments around slogan awareness as a research assistant in a consumer psychology laboratory. In fact, those roles played a key part in switching my major from engineering to organizational psychology, which led me to adopt a steady studying routine that earned me a spot on the other dean's list, finishing college with close to a 3.5 grade point average (yes, I had to achieve almost straight As at that point to get there). I had navigated a few paths based on having an oar in many waters. It was not a direct route but a variety of experiences that led me to an engaging life path. What I failed to realize then was that I had the capabilities to succeed, but I was not aligned with clear goals and often not deeply engaged in something I was passionate about.

After getting my bachelor's degree, I wasn't sure if I should go right to work or continue on for an advanced degree. Should I get married to someone I had been dating for several years? Was it too early in my life? Should I continue my musical interests with a band called DeSade? We had been asked to go on a limited national tour, but what would this do to my career trajectory and my life fulfillment?

I tried several jobs—recruiter, editor, real estate agent, and even a night shift keypunch operator. (How many of you know what that is? The answer: a keypunch operator was someone who punched codes into computer cards that in turn were fed into a huge mainframe computer for processing.) However, those jobs were not aligned with my values, underutilized my skills, and did not engage me.

Finally, I sought an advanced degree that would keep me close to my girlfriend while I sorted out where I wanted to go from there. Ultimately, I realized that my dream life would combine my dream girlfriend and the interests that remained in my wheelhouse. So I asked her to marry me (thank goodness she said yes!), and we began planning our joint career paths together, which ultimately took us to graduate work in Illinois.

My next great nexus was choosing among a narrower band of options: teacher, researcher, or practitioner. I started that decision path with a visiting teaching role at the University of Iowa and then expanded my research and teaching options with a full-time role at Georgia Tech. Despite my love of research and teaching, which my graduate degree in organizational psychology prepared me for, somehow at age twenty-seven I still felt unfulfilled. I wanted to live the theories I was teaching at Georgia Tech—to test those theories in real organizations. But even after my transition to a major tele-communications firm that afforded me a chance to combine both research and practice, I still felt something was missing. Perhaps I was missing the teaching element and the ability to influence many as opposed to few. I found what I was looking for, along with my strong entrepreneurial interests, in a job offer to lead a research practice for a global consulting organization.

This role prepared me for a transition—the creation of the Metrus Group, which would last twenty-eight years (so far!)—that has created deep enjoyment and personal fulfillment for me. This career choice blends my keen enjoyment of research and analytics with my entrepreneurial and leadership skills while also giving me the opportunity to work with and make practical changes at hundreds of real organizations. The satisfaction of making a difference is not unique to me; it is one of the most fervently voiced desires of scores of interviewees we talked to on this journey to discover fulfillment. But I had to find my own way to make a difference—one that capitalized on who I was and where I wanted to go. And it took me until age thirty-nine to discover my dream career.

I begin by talking about career satisfaction because it is the number one element of life fulfillment for the majority of people that I interviewed in my research. The second most important element of life fulfillment for the majority of my respondents consists of their relationships, typically those with a primary friend or spouse, supported by a network of other relationships. My relationship challenges included deep thinking about who should be part of my life, the timing of my marriage, whether to have children, and so forth. I realized that for me, I could not have achieved the turnaround in college or the professional success I have garnered over the years without a spouse who has been a great complement to me. (She does compliment me, but not too much—to "keep my head from swelling," as she says.)

My journey to life fulfillment is not atypical. Some of this journey was necessary to discover life's lessons, but many parts were not. I wasted periods of time going down blind alleys. I taxied through many roles without truly taking off. I drifted dangerously close to academic or career waterfalls that could have drowned me. As I reflected on much of this and my experience with people like Marisa, I set out to discover if there was a more effective and rewarding way to reach one's dreams.

What Is Fulfillment?

Psychologist and researcher Martin Seligman of the University of Pennsylvania is often seen as the father of the field of positive psychology, turning our eyes toward the full glass rather than the glass half empty. Rather than focusing on clinical dysfunctions, he, and now many other psychologists, has focused on what makes us satisfied, happy, or even delighted.[5]

While I began my own work with an eye toward how individuals and organizations come together for win-win outcomes, the research and many interviews conducted for this book shifted its direction to a broader issue of fulfillment—an enduring quality that includes both daily happiness and, more important, a long-term, sustainable sense of achieving all one can be. Most of my interviewees talked about the difference between fleeting wins such as a pay raise, promotion, or even winning the lottery (yes, research shows that even that is fleeting) and a long-term sense of purpose and accomplishment in their lives.

So when someone asks me if fulfillment means satisfaction, happiness, success, achievement, or inner peace, I say yes, because it must be compounded of a variety of factors. I define *life fulfillment* as *achieving one's dreams and creating a lifestyle that brings exceptional happiness and inner peace.* An adjunct to this is being all one can be. Perfect fulfillment is rarely achieved. It is an ideal that most of us seek. The most fulfilled people seem to be closer to that dream than others. That is good news for us and probably part of our biological makeup, because if we were totally fulfilled, we would stop growing, developing, learning, and adapting to the world around us. In short, we would stagnate, pulling us off our Mount Olympus of fulfillment.

There has been a good deal of work on many of the concepts I mention here, but what is absent by and large is how we plan to get to fulfillment. Much research shows we need to feel a sense of control over our destiny in order to achieve happiness (even if only in our own mind). Some societies and organizations, for a variety of economic and social reasons, create environments in which people feel a greater sense of control, resulting in greater happiness and a variety of other positive outcomes. But regardless of the context, individuals can proactively increase their control through their actions.

This book addresses some of the key factors that enable you to have greater control and influence over your life—factors such as having a clear vision of the future, having a life path, being planful and resourceful, understanding your success drivers, managing today's actions to get you to tomorrow, having a personal scorecard to track your progress, and employing lessons learned from others that enable you to bypass some of life's cul-de-sacs.

Life is about choices, but life is also filled with randomness that we must respond to. Most fulfilled people are adept at making good choices along life's path and adapting to the inevitable setbacks that almost all of them have experienced along the way. That fulfillment is in part due to their understanding of who they are—as both emotional and rational beings—and also taking an active role in planning their lives.

The approach suggested in this book may help marry the rational thinking of our left brain—goals, skills, facts—with the emotional needs and interests of our right brain in the search for happiness and fulfillment. This requires self-awareness, planning, making choices, taking stock of where you are, and being honest and realistic. The framework in this book will help you think through choices and make conscious decisions about work, family, community, volunteerism, and other situations. You will also learn about the personal scorecard, a central tool for translating vision and plans into everyday behaviors that lead to fulfillment.

We all want to be successful, but more important, we want to feel fulfilled. Unless success is in the context of a vision, it may feel fleeting. Success is often attached to things: getting a promotion, making more money, getting that special person to say yes, or winning the lottery. Even top executives that I interviewed—people with money, fame, and power—are not all happy or fulfilled. The money, fame, or power did not always bring about fulfillment.

Not all of us achieve fulfillment in the same way, which is fortunate; the world could not support ten thousand Gandhis or Olympic gold medalists, three hundred million social workers, or seventeen thousand congressmen and congresswomen (thank goodness). Fulfillment requires adaptation. With the increasing pace of change in today's world, standing still is not an option. With increasing globalization, greater opportunities for social and geographic mobility, a panoply of educational options, and a wide variety of social and cultural values, the sky is the limit—but only for those who plan effectively and execute those plans. Too often, people end up as victims of their own lack of goals, indecision, or poor choices along the way.

It was also exciting to learn that the techniques used by those who are most fulfilled are easily transferrable to people who are open to hearing them. I was fortunate to eventually arrive at a pretty exciting place in my life after a winding path, but our research team has interviewed many who have bounced from college major to major, job to job, or relationship to relationship without discovering the deep satisfaction of fulfillment. No, you cannot guarantee someone a perfect road to fulfillment, but you can increase the odds greatly! Let's explore this concept together.

This book is not about becoming rich. It is not about becoming famous. It is not about becoming a star in your profession. It is about becoming fulfilled in all aspects of your life. This may include your profession, your relationships, your education, your hobbies, and many more life aspects. This book is for anyone at any age who is willing to learn. It is never too early—or too late—to think about what makes you fulfilled. It is never too late to start becoming fulfilled. I have watched friends blossom in retirement and enjoy life in new and profound ways: my wife's grandfather began an artistic career when he was over sixty-five and went on to be admired for his portraits and seascapes.

If you are looking for a happier and more rewarding life, this book is for you. If you are a coach or mentor, this book will give you insights into helping others. And if you are a human resources or organizational leader, this book should provide insights into how you can attract, develop, optimize, and retain the best talent—talent that will find your organization and its culture rewarding in their personal journey to fulfillment. Too often, those who study organizations shy away from the overlapping sphere of personal space for career, counseling, and clinical psychology. When individual and organizational alignment occurs, individuals feel fulfilled and organizations benefit from outstanding performance—a win-win for all.

I hope to help you understand many of the factors that drive success, happiness, and satisfaction and encourage you to take charge of these factors in an effective way on your journey to short- and long-term fulfillment. Every minute you sit on the sidelines is a minute lost.

Let's make it happen.

Your Guide through the Book

In Part I, I share examples of highly successful versus less successful people. It has questions and answers. What is different between the two cases? What's going on in the world that makes this proactive approach essential, not optional? In Part II, I take a look at the critical elements of fulfillment and examine the ingredients that are common to most fulfilled people, regardless of their profession. This provides a context for thinking about what makes us feel fulfilled. In Part III, I turn to the "science" of fulfillment. Borrowing many tools used in business today, I address the stages of building a successful life plan, from setting life goals to measuring yourself. Businesses have used a variety of techniques such as balanced scorecards, contingency planning, and goal setting to achieve high performance and success. Why shouldn't you apply these techniques to your life planning? Each chapter will address one of the key stages that you can apply to your own life plan.

Part III may be of special interest to millennials who are just beginning their lives and career paths. It offers fairly detailed guidance about how to identify intermediate, "lighthouse goals" and link them to the values, drivers, and life plan that will represent fulfillment to you. However, there is nothing wrong with skipping ahead to Part IV, which discusses the "art" of becoming fulfilled. In this section, I look at how those with long-term fulfillment have dealt with setbacks, recovered from bad decisions, avoided life's cul-de-sacs, and employed key success factors to get where they are today.

Why do diet or exercise plans fall apart? Why do only 8 percent of people complete their New Year's resolutions?[6] This part will address how you can overcome the risks and challenges as well as examine some of the tools and techniques employed by fulfillment "stars." Also throughout this book are worksheets to use in your thinking, planning, and action.

PART I

THE CHALLENGE

1

Mack, Mary, and Emil

People take different roads seeking fulfillment and happiness.
Just because they're not on your road does not mean they are lost.
—Dalai Lama

When a child is born today in the most economically developed parts of the globe, he or she is likely to have nearly 34 million minutes to spend on earth—more than 41 million if the child grows up in the United States or another highly developed country. When you remove approximately 2.6 million minutes in which one is too young to be aware of that window of opportunity and approximately 10.7 million minutes in which no one has much control over their life, such as during sleep, that leaves just a little more than 21 million minutes—quite an allotment of time to achieve your life fulfillment, *or not*. The question is how wisely those minutes are spent.

Take Mack, who is seventy-five and sees himself as highly fulfilled. Mack feels delighted every day. He is retired from a long career with a manufacturing company, where he had some good and bad bosses. He has a loving family and many close friends, and he is friendly with his neighbors and many other members of his community. Despite the long hours at his previous job, Mack found time to volunteer throughout his life. For many years, he served a community volunteer fire company. Serving others seemed to be part of the family DNA—his wife helped children with disabilities. Mack always found time to talk with his neighbors, and despite his challenging schedule, he loved to mow his lawn even though he could have had his son or neighbors do it.

Contrast Mack with Mary, who is miserable at forty-five. She has lived life through everyone else's expectations. Her parents were well educated and had high hopes for her to achieve success in a respectable profession. She had aunts and uncles with many accomplishments. She had a parent-driven education program, and getting less than an A was simply unacceptable. While she excelled in school throughout her law degree, she nearly dropped out. She really didn't like law (or medicine, her father's preference); she actually liked theater and art. As a young adult, she tried to become part of a local theater troupe and take acting classes. Her parents dissuaded her, as did her husband when she talked about giving up law. After having a child she was unsure about having, she felt trapped because of her family's financial situation. Mary took on the weight of others' expectations instead of her own and saw her options collapsing. She didn't have a vision for her own life, clear goals, or a way to manage her past and current dilemmas. She focused on what didn't happen instead of what could still happen.

Or look at Emil, now fifty, who has three kids who have left the nest. Looking back, all Emil can remember is getting married, followed by a whirlwind of child raising—preschool classes, shuttling his kids and their friends to games, communions, confirmations, and graduations. Then they were gone. He is now depressed, feeling as if he is just waiting for the end. He has succumbed to social stereotypes about being "over the hill." The comic Brian Regan talks about building a ramp when he was a kid. He and his friends would ride their bikes up the ramp, totally forgetting to finish the plan for what they would do when they were in midair. The story ends with one of the kids going to the hospital. Rather than focusing on the potential for his future, Emil got caught in a parallel situation; he planned for the job and three kids—but then what's at the end of his ramp? He didn't have a life plan with long-term goals and a balanced portfolio of fulfilling activities. Now he dwells in the past. Emil still has well over seven million minutes of nonsleeping existence ahead of him, on average. Can he find fulfillment in his remaining years?

Life Is Not a Recipe

There is no magic pill to life satisfaction, just as there is no one way to bake a cake, prepare a gourmet dinner, or enjoy a sunset. This was driven home to me in a course that my wife and I took with a famous master chef, Craig Shelton, himself a protégé of several French master chefs. While we took a cooking class with Craig, he was being filmed by a public broadcasting network and was the first chef to appear on the cover of *Gourmet Magazine*. Craig could have become a well-known TV chef or the owner of a chain of restaurants bearing his name, but Craig is not a typical chef.

For starters, he has a PhD in biochemistry. He approaches food not as a collection of recipes to be copied religiously but as an ongoing experiment to be savored. His chemistry background enables him to think outside the box about the building blocks of cuisine, whether simple *pommes frites* (sounds more exciting than French fries, no?) or the preparation of duck. As students in Chef Shelton's class, we learned we didn't need a PhD, but we did need to think about a variety of sciences that support having a great meal—emulsion, the science that creates a great vinaigrette; how all proteins (whether from eggs, meat, or beans, depending on your veggie bent) must be gently nudged to their prime texture; and how to create flavor combinations with herbs and spices. While at first this seemed like it might be daunting, in short order we found that by learning these basic food science principles, we were soon throwing away all our recipes and making unique and wonderful meals.

Most of us like to eat a wonderful meal, just as most of us want a fulfilling life made up of many satisfying days. By thinking about the science of life fulfillment and honing the ingredients in ways that fit us best, we create our own savory life banquet. Some people in our class did not like the spiciness of Indian food. For others, it was not spicy enough. Still others were more meat-and-potato fans. And yet, as we spent our evenings eating meals that we or the staff had cooked using culinary principles, we opened our eyes to new and exciting tastes. My wife and I had never had many of the combinations that were created, but by applying the chef's principles and using fresh ingredients, we (and everyone in the class) savored the experience each week.

Most important, we left the class equipped to whip up our own wonderful concoctions, whether we were spice lovers, salad grazers, meat cravers, or dessert junkies. The same could be said of life. Some of us are workaholics, travel trekkies, soccer fanatics, legal beagles, or opera aficionados.

LIFE HAS MANY COMPENSATORY ELEMENTS

Let's follow the cuisine example a little further because it is a good metaphor for life's choices. Chef Shelton didn't stop at simply preparing tasty food; he said food alone is not enough. Most of the diners in his highly starred restaurant enjoyed wine as well. Unfortunately, a fair number of his customers didn't know much about wine (or food), but their wallets often gave them the confidence to order whatever struck their fancy. The wine and food were not always well paired, creating a risk that the food that tasted marvelous in the kitchen would seem bitter or sweet or dull when eaten with a misaligned wine match.

Did Chef Shelton come out and give them a lesson? No, although I'm sure he was tempted. One Saturday night in the kitchen, we watched him shudder when he inspected the wine and food ordered at a particular table. We thought he was going to become apoplectic. What could he do about parties that would ruin his food or wine? But he believed that everyone should optimize their flavor and tasting experience, and because of his chemistry background, he realized that he would have to change ingredients behind the scenes in his kitchen "lab" to compensate for their ill-advised wine pairings. We learned in our class that we could use spices, herbs, and cooking styles to compensate for mediocre wine matches and still give the diner a wonderful outcome. But the lesson for us was that pairings are important. We can compensate for some poor pairings, but not all, such as serving an overpowering Zinfandel with a Dover sole.

And this is true for most things in life. We can perhaps blend a job with long hours and child rearing by finding quality time with a child. I tried to find time to bond with my nephews, who lived in distant cities, by bringing them to visit periodically and doing something special when I had the time with them. They still talk about the once-in-a-lifetime experience we had at a Cape Canaveral space shuttle launch. Quality memories can be perhaps more important than the total amount of time we have with loved ones.

Other pairings might include developing incredibly exciting hobbies to balance a less-than-interesting job. My wife and I learned bridge from one such individual who was not exactly stimulated by his routine work but was exhilarated by teaching others to excel at bridge. He organized tournaments, ran classes, and brought enjoyment to many; it was clear that this aspect of his life was quite fulfilling. His entire body became animated when he was in his groove or "flow," as recent research has described it. Flow is the ability to lose oneself completely when immersed in something totally engaging.

Think of other pairings or areas of balance in your own life. Are there things that you do to excess in one area that need balance in another?

FOCUS ON ELEMENTS BUT LIVE IN THE WHOLE

This leads me to one final insight about our chef. He did not stop with food and wine. He said the experience of coming to his restaurant was of paramount importance. It had not only outstanding food and a great wine selection but an ambiance that made one feel great. There was a friendly greeter at the front door, not the haughty receptionist some of us have experienced at expensive restaurants. The experience included a great smile from the maître d', a nod from a busboy, a quick and friendly opening with an *amuse-bouche* from the kitchen, and often a personal hello from the chef as he quickly toured the dining rooms.

Earlier in our lives, my wife and I ate at a restaurant owned by two brothers. They eventually went their separate ways. One brother created an over-the-top dining establishment that made many people feel as if they were being judged by their wine and cuisine choices and expertise. The other created a friendly atmosphere combined with the same great cuisine; it grew and prospered as diners enjoyed the entire experience without feeling judged. Even if the food and wine are superb, people want to have an experience that makes them feel good.

The same is true in life. We all want a rich life experience, not just a job, a meal, an acquaintance, or a hobby. We want the things we do to have meaning. Ultimately, we need to combine the elements of our lives in a way that brings us fulfillment.

In this book, I will address some easy and important things that you can do to set the table for a fulfilling life:

- understanding what fulfillment is and is not
- identifying what separates those who are fulfilled from those who are not
- learning about the "science" of fulfillment—the principles that enable you to plan, decide, and take action that will bring fulfillment
- applying the "art" of fulfillment—the lessons from highly fulfilled people that you can apply to your life

This book may take you a few hours to read, but I hope it will provide a lifetime of fulfillment.

2

How Fulfilled Are You?

The good life is using your signature strengths every day to produce authentic happiness and abundant gratification.
—Martin Seligman, *Authentic Happiness: Using the New Positive Psychology to Realize Your Potential for Lasting Fulfillment*

Before we dig into the ingredients of fulfillment, I think you will find it helpful if you assess how fulfilled you are today. Here is a short questionnaire (fig. 1). If you would rather access it online, see http://www.wschiemann.com/fulfilled. Mark how you feel about each statement in the first column using the scale of "Strongly Agree" to "Strongly Disagree."

FIGURE 1. How Fulfilled Are You?

	Strongly Disagree	Disagree	Neutral	Agree	Strongly Agree
I have a life purpose and clear goals.	1	2	3	4	5
I feel successful with my job and career.	1	2	3	4	5
I am satisfied with the relationships in my life.	1	2	3	4	5

(continued)

FIGURE 1. How Fulfilled Are You? (*continued*)

	Strongly Disagree	Disagree	Neutral	Agree	Strongly Agree
Most days, I can act consistently with my inner values.	1	2	3	4	5
I have one or more hobbies or spiritual activities that bring me enjoyment.	1	2	3	4	5
I spend most of my days satisfied.	1	2	3	4	5
When I have setbacks from my goals or plans, I know how to turn that around to my advantage.	1	2	3	4	5
I am healthy.	1	2	3	4	5
I have sufficient education, skills, and experiences to do what I want to do in life.	1	2	3	4	5
I have a way to measure my life fulfillment.	1	2	3	4	5

TOTAL ALIGNMENT _____
Score (add up your score for the questions)

Add the numbers you chose. If you score higher than 45, you are one of the lucky few who are highly fulfilled. If you score between 35 and 44, you are moderately fulfilled. If you score is below 35, there are many things you can do to become more highly fulfilled, which I will address in the following chapters of this book. As you will see, these statements cover some of the key factors that drive life fulfillment for a majority of us.

In the first chapter, I gave a few examples of fulfillment. Let's take a look at a couple of examples from different walks of life to help us understand what distinguishes those who are fulfilled from those who are not.

RENE'S REGRET

Rene is a senior manager with a large pharmaceutical company. He did not discover how to find fulfillment until midlife. After one marriage that didn't go well and a career of jumping from place to place, coupled with a frantic home life, he realized that he wasn't getting older and wiser but older and less fulfilled. He said that he really didn't stop to smell the roses; instead, he raced from one task to the next.

After a missed job opportunity, he decided to reassess, to take a "time out." He had always been intrigued with yoga and meditation. He decided that his time out would include adding more of these activities and reflection into his daily life. The time out didn't last very long, but it gave him new insights into his life goals and what he wanted to accomplish—his bucket list, if you will. He also fundamentally changed his routines, giving himself an hour each morning to meditate. While that meant getting up earlier, he felt more energized than before, and slowly he began to adopt new behaviors, rediscovering the world around him. His relationships improved; he began to take a portion of his day to volunteer and to truly listen to others around him.

His only lament was, "I wish I could have discovered this sooner. So many lost hours were wasted." But he knows that his future will be a different story, with more job and relationship satisfaction and life fulfillment. Since his change, he has turned down two lucrative offers for top-level positions at other firms. He remarked that those positions would be like jumping back into the rat race he had escaped from. He quipped, "If you are fulfilled, then what will you gain by such moves?"

Rene was successful because he focused on his goals and the activities that brought him fulfillment. He was able to translate that into his daily routine as well as develop a clear vision of the future. When thinking about his enticing new job offers, it took him a millisecond to respond "no" because he had a clear vision of what "yes" was.

CAROL'S CHOICE

Carol had been brought up in a conservative Midwestern town. Marriage was a sacred institution. In college she met a conservative boy, the son of an established Midwestern family. What's more, he was on a trajectory to become a headmaster at a small school. The stars seemed aligned, and they were married. But Carol soon realized she was not cut out to be a headmaster's wife. She was bright, energetic, ambitious, and increasingly outspoken—not the model headmaster's wife where they lived. The community expected her to be subservient and to simply be there to support her husband and the school.

Carol was a good soldier at first. They lived on a modest salary and tried to raise two children in a community that was increasingly affluent. Carol's career ambitions had been stifled. She realized that her problem was misalignment between her career aspirations and her daily routine. While many of her values were aligned with her husband and the school, her aspirations and desired style of living were not. She became increasingly unhappy, and after a long period of suffering, she finally said she had to get out. She didn't want to hurt her husband, their children, or the school, but it was either survive and thrive or stay in place and wither.

They divorced and she took an entry job in a communications company. Suddenly, she felt a sense of personal mastery—a sense of competence that she had not felt for more than a decade. She could do valuable things! Her career soared quickly, and she became a well-paid professional with a great deal of responsibility. She thrived on it because it was aligned with her inner self. It allowed her to add value in new ways and unleash her creativity. She had an encouraging boss who also brought out the best in her. He recognized her and supported her development, leading to a level of engagement with her work that surprised even her. She didn't mind working long hours because she was loving it. As she settled into her new life, she was then able to go back and refocus on her children in a new way, using her new financial resources to provide experiences for them that she could not afford earlier.

Carol's change included three key elements. She became more aligned with her vision and values, she was able to demonstrate competence, and she was energized or engaged with her job, boss, and company. We will talk more about these three elements later.

VICTOR'S AWAKENING

Carol's husband, Victor, was very much in love with her and deeply depressed when she made the life-transforming move. At first, he was sure she would come to her senses and return. He could not understand why she wanted to do the things she was doing. Sure, the money was better, but she had to work so many hours. She was enduring a long commute. She didn't get to see the kids every day (he remained the guardian of the children). Sure, he knew she was frustrated, especially in the last year or so, but didn't they have the most important things?

What Victor didn't see was the lack of alignment in the way they each looked at the world and how they achieved fulfillment. He felt more fulfilled having achieved the career he chose, being respected by the community, giving to others, and enjoying his social interactions. He was gregarious by nature, and the role allowed him to leverage that strength. But after Carol's departure, he too came to grips with some misalignments in his life. He realized that his commitment to the school was too one-sided, with the community taking but not returning all the energy he needed. His kids were growing up; he valued them and would need more money to put them through school. He also began to realize that what he had thought was high simpatico with Carol was instead perhaps routine and codependence.

He met another woman after a few years who knocked him off his feet. She was socially outgoing—a better match to his style than Carol. She enjoyed parties and had similar hobbies and interests. She brought out new energies in him. He subsequently left his educational career and started a business as an entrepreneur. He was proud of his new and growing competencies in the business—more than I had seen before. He admitted to me one day that he had been mistaken about Carol; he was far more aligned with his new wife in so many ways. Yes, they had been married for almost twenty years, but he began to realize that he had been unconsciously forcing Carol to fit his mold—a mold that suited him at the time—while depleting her.

In the end, both Carol and Victor achieved higher alignment with their life goals, found jobs and roles that allowed them to leverage their competencies, and found life situations—jobs, hobbies, relationships—that energized or engaged them, resulting in far higher fulfillment.

So what is this concept of fulfillment? We have defined life fulfillment as achieving one's dreams and creating a lifestyle that brings exceptional happiness and inner peace. An adjunct to this is being all one can be because to be less is to have unfulfilled potential, which is not only a waste of your capabilities but a loss for society as a whole.

Rene, Carol, and Victor eventually found fulfillment after decades of frustration and unhappiness. Each of them had the potential to be fulfilled earlier in their lives if they had applied some of the tools and thinking that we will cover throughout the book:

- understanding three critical ingredients to fulfillment
- applying the science of becoming fulfilled
- becoming adept at the art of fulfillment

WHAT ARE THE INGREDIENTS OF FULFILLMENT?

In the previous chapter, we learned about restaurateur Craig Shelton and how he created a fulfilling restaurant for both the proprietor as well as the patrons. Another famous chef, Danny Meyer, using a different model, created restaurants as diverse as the Union Square Cafe and the Shake Shack—a fast-food emporium that had New Yorkers queuing up in long lines to wait for, well, the ubiquitous burger.[1] His decade-old experiment, now being mimicked in many other cities, demonstrated that certain fine dining principles, such as premium, fresh ingredients and service, can be profitably applied at even the margin-thin quick-serve level. What are the right ingredients that will go into your fulfillment?

Three of the most important ingredients are called ACE, and I will explore them with you in Part II. We discovered ACE in our work with organizations and found that these ingredients of success were applicable for both organizations and individuals. Are we Aligned, Capable, and Engaged in what we do and where we are going in life? People who are high on ACE feel more fulfilled in their lives; they stay in jobs longer, are more productive, report less stress in their lives, and have other positive feelings. We will explore why that happens and how you can increase the ACE in your life.

You will learn what it means to be a high ACE individual. Carol's and Victor's stories contain the ingredients for high fulfillment—alignment with their interests, aptitudes, and values; having the "right" capabilities to be successful along the way; and being engaged or energized in what they do. ACE can be applied to both work and nonwork aspects of your life.

THE SCIENCE OF FULFILLMENT

Most of us don't think about the words *fulfillment* and *science* in the same mental sphere. But there is actually a set of principles that underlie the road to fulfillment. Each of these principles is accompanied by a set of tools that can be used to plan for and manage your life fulfillment. The principles are not "rocket science" per se but elude many people because of habits, distractions, or missing skills that could be readily improved. Let's take a look at the primary ones.

- Clear life goals: Where would you like to end up by the end of your life? Will you have created the value that is important both to you and to society? What will you be remembered for?

- A set of drivers: What are the actions or elements that cause high versus low fulfillment? (These are often missed.)
- A life map: Do you have a visual representation of how your life goals connect to where you are today so that you can plan and invest your time wisely?
- Life sensors: What are some ways to measure where you are along the way? (A personal scorecard is one example.)
- A life plan including a strategy for achieving your life goals: How do you determine what will get you to where you want to go?

THE ART OF FULFILLMENT

There is also the art of becoming fulfilled. While I'm sure that many of us could read a book on running a restaurant, if we applied the scientific principles rigidly, we would probably fail, having missed the art of success. Think about one of your favorite artists—Renoir, Adams, Rembrandt, Braque, or Picasso. With a paint-by-number kit, we could more or less reproduce the basics of one of their pictures, but would it be great art? Hardly. The brush strokes, layering, perspective, and many other fine touches must come together to create great art.

While the science will provide the basic principles and supporting tools for creating a life-fulfilling plan, it will be the judgments, decisions, and appropriate applications of those principles that make your life truly fulfilling. Can you avoid roadblocks? Are there short-cuts? How do you recover when derailed? These are the tricks of the trade that we only learn from those who are fulfilled or discover through the long and painful process of trial and error.

Do you remember starting a new job? (Or if you have not had one yet, imagine starting one.) Remember all the things in your training and prior experiences that enabled you to succeed. These were the ingredients of success. Then there were all of the things that you were told by the hiring manager and other interviewers that would be important to success—hitting certain performance targets or goals, living the company values, applying high-quality principles of your trade, using the right measures, listening for performance feedback, and so forth. In many ways, these were the formal steps, or science, of success. But then you probably talked to a few coworkers the first week who began to share the hidden rules of success. It may have been things like "don't contradict the boss," "don't outshine the team," "volunteer for special projects," and the like. This is the art of success—street smarts versus book learning.

The same is true of finding fulfillment. Yes, there are principles or steps (the science, so to speak) that will help you realize your vision. But it will also take some art and finesse: lessons we have learned from others who have already traveled this road and have achieved fulfillment. Those tips—the art—along with the science of fulfillment will take you a long way toward your goals.

BRIDGET'S STORY

Let's take a deeper look at one individual who is feeling overwhelmed on her journey of life. Bridget is a recent college graduate. She is in the last stages of earning her master's but is frustrated and unsure about what steps to take next. Should she enter the workforce? Would seeking a PhD be right for her? Would she prefer to work for a large or small corporation? What about a consulting firm? Or should she consider joining her brother, who wants to start a small business?

There is a world of opportunity available for Bridget; however, she must find her own path. As we've seen from our previous stories, the right path is not always the first one we try, or the easiest. As we progress through this book, we will explore along with Bridget some of the crucial decisions that will help her write the next pages of her book of life. While there is no one-size-fits-all solution to career fulfillment, as we'll see, there are many steps Bridget can take to try to find the ACE within her. However, I will share two cautionary notes before we move on.

Life Fulfillment Is a Probability

Think about people who gamble. Some people like to bet on Powerball—hitting it big with a mega jackpot—even though the odds are a million to one that they will succeed. Others who have great memories for counting cards may play blackjack, a game that provides one of the best odds for beating the house. These folks often win a good deal of the time. They rarely win super-big, but they win steadily.

If you think that you are not a gambler, think again. We all gamble, but in different ways. We gamble with our investment of time. We bet that a certain investment of our time will bring us what we want. While nothing is guaranteed, this book and the principles it describes will increase your odds for fulfillment. The more life-fulfilling principles you observe, the higher your probability of fulfillment.

We operate in a complex, highly changing world of economics, politics, social relationships, job and career opportunities, and uncertain health. It would be a mistake to say, "If I create this plan and manage this process, fulfillment is guaranteed." Instead, one should look at this the way a sports team would: "If we have a good strategy, develop the right skills, train well, have a good game plan and monitor our performance so we can adjust going forward, we will win a higher percentage of our games."

As the old adage goes, on any given Sunday, anyone might win or lose, but as we learned from the best seller *Moneyball*, science can help us increase our odds. You can't do better than that. Furthermore, fulfillment is in the eyes of the beholder. With regard to that Sunday football game, one person is fulfilled by being the player on the field, another by coaching, and another by sitting on the couch and watching as a major form of relaxation. While that game on Sunday is only one of thousands of individual activities that these three people may do in their lives, if it is part of a balanced life philosophy that creates fulfillment, those individual activities may all be just as important to the persons engaged in doing them. On the other hand, if you dread every moment of playing football (it is just a way to get a paycheck) or you dread every moment of coaching (but do it because you were talked into it), participating in those activities is not a productive way to move you toward life fulfillment.

DON'T OBSESS

A second caution is one of return on investment of your time. Many people working for a sizable employer have some financial investments—perhaps through their employer's 401(k) or other plans. It is prudent to have a financial strategy that includes things like how you will pay for today's expenses and the kids' education and still have money left for your retirement and health needs. Experts recommend talking to a financial advisor and building a good plan. But most of us don't want to watch the financial markets every day, hour, or minute. We have financial firms that do that for us. The key is having a financial goal, a plan for how to achieve that goal, and periodic measures that enable us to see if the plan is on track.

Managing life fulfillment is similar. Once you create a good plan and set it in motion, your time should be spent on doing the things that will fulfill you, while periodically measuring how well that plan is working. It should not take more time than enjoying your sense of fulfillment. Don't be like people I met recently at a ski resort, who were more obsessed with how many vertical feet they had skied each day than with the enjoyment of the skiing experience.

While the processes described in this book are a great guide and will require more work in the beginning to get you off to a rousing start, over time these principles should become simply a way you think, review, and revise your life.

PART II

THE ACE IN YOU

I thought I would enjoy working at a company with a social mission, but I didn't realize what a huge difference it would make. I can feel the difference in my attitude and motivations about my job. This is what work is supposed to be about.

—DonorsChoose.org

One Monday morning, a colleague of mine was in a wonderful mood. She said she had the most exhilarating weekend. When I asked what had made her weekend so exhilarating, she said that she had blended many of the activities she loved to do. Keri spent time with her kids, went to a baseball game, went shopping, had a delightful dinner on Saturday night, watched a movie, took an aerobics class, caught up on her paperwork, and luxuriated in a long bath. And, if that wasn't enough, she also reviewed a recent business article and proofed a report for a client. The opportunity to combine and coordinate her favorite activities was wonderful. When she added, "It's too bad work isn't like that most of the time," it got me thinking.

Kurt, a friend of mine, has a different story. Kurt thrives on his work—closing a deal, tackling and solving new work-related problems, and schmoozing with a client over a beer. His problem is balancing that with the other areas of his life. His first marriage, I sensed, fell apart due to his constant preoccupation with work. He had not developed hobbies or much of a social life, and the constant stress of work—and only work—took its toll.

What was it about Keri's great weekend that was so much more exhilarating than a day at work? And what was so compelling about Kurt's work that he let it drown out other aspects of his life? Is there a right balance?

During a conversation with Keri, I discovered that the things she did over that weekend represented different segments of her life that brought her fulfillment. For her, it was the variety of things that she immersed herself in that made the difference, with few distasteful activities. Kurt, on the other hand, loved one aspect of his life but felt that he was unbalanced in some way, leading to feelings of dread when he was not working. I wondered how we could integrate work and nonwork activities into our lives in such a way that the overall balance is as close to exhilarating as one can get. After many years of research, I got my answer by looking at both individuals and organizations and how they optimize the one common commodity that they all have: time.

Think about other ways that we optimize our lives—trying to get the most of our weekend by balancing sports events, kids' programs, exercise, TV time, eating a great meal, and making time for a hobby, such as gardening or rebuilding a car. When organizations try to optimize their talent, they are doing something similar: they are trying to find the right mix of experiences, abilities, interests, and behaviors in the pursuit of the organization's vision and goals.

How do we leverage the time and ability of a fast-food employee with the equipment provided to maximize the service experience of the customer? And how does the fast-food employer balance training, communication, and incentives to create knowing and caring employees who come to work eager to delight customers? How can someone in a product-development role successfully balance his or her time among inventing new products, staying current in the latest technology, and recharging innovative brain cells when not inventing work-related products? How do companies leverage the time of busy executives, and how do they help those executives balance other areas in their lives in order to give them the patience to coach employees, deal with stressful situations, and reach productivity goals?

For example, think of the last time you checked into a hotel. You wanted impeccable service, including a quick and efficient check-in and a room with the amenities you requested. But much goes on behind the scenes: desk staff members must be trained to be pleasant and effective, the computer reservation system must extract your reservation correctly and quickly, and some logistics person has to allocate room types in a way that allows you to get the room with the queen-size beds that you prefer. In essence, the hotel must optimize its talent—the skills, experiences, and knowledge of the desk clerk—with its computer and planning processes to try to satisfy you at check-in.

The same concept can be applied to our own lives, as Keri's example highlights. How do we create the right mix of work, family, hobbies, and other key areas of our lives that will give us optimal fulfillment? In selecting a career or job, what mix of activities will create the most enjoyment and satisfaction for you?

WORK IS IMPORTANT FOR MOST

In our interviews with people, we found that work is a strong factor in determining life fulfillment. While the part-time "gig economy" is growing, and there are many entrepreneurs, a majority of people still work full time in organizations. So while many of my stories will pertain to the organizational environment, the principles in this book are equally applicable to all types of work, relationships, and avocations. Former EEOC chairman Gil Casellas said, "We spend so much of our life at work or commuting to work that the majority of our waking hours are connected to work. That is why it is so important for companies to build cultures that are fulfilling."

Research from the Metrus Institute tells us that only about 20 percent of the departments in more than two thousand organizations that were studied have done a good job of optimizing their investments in people—that is, they are getting the most energy and performance for the money they are investing in talent. Just think of the waste in business today: people working long hours on low-priority projects that will never see the light of day, employees struggling to satisfy customers without sufficient training to do so, and managers squelching the excitement that an employee first brings to work. These are just a few of the ways in which we sub-optimize the precious talent that organizations have available in their people.

At the beginning of this book, I mentioned that there are many learnings from business that can be applied to our personal lives and in particular to fulfillment. In this chapter and the next part of the book, I will share some of these with you. In this chapter, I will first shed light on how some of these concepts are used from the organizational point of view before I show you how to use them to your advantage as an individual.

In my work with Metrus, I discovered a concept we coined "People Equity." It has been powerful in helping us understand how well people and their talents can be optimized in organizations—in other words, being all they can be. People Equity is composed of three factors that are crucial to optimizing talent—you and me—in organizations, abbreviated as ACE (an acronym for Alignment, Capabilities, Engagement). Examples of these factors include:

- people who are *aligned* with the organization's goals, its values, its customers and others with whom they work
- people who have the "right" *capabilities*—the competencies, information, and resources—to meet or exceed customer or client expectations
- people who are *engaged* with the organization—and are willing to put in additional effort as needed to accomplish goals, willing to recommend the organization as a place to work, and willing to volunteer for special projects at work, or in the community

Collectively, we have labeled these three ACE factors People Equity. I will first discuss how we use ACE in a company or organization environment, but these principles hold equally true if you are an entrepreneur, a student experiencing an academic environment, a home manager, or someone creating a community environment.

When an organization has high People Equity (ACE), Metrus has found that:

- organizations are more profitable or reach their goals more effectively
- customers are more loyal and buy more
- employees stay with the organization longer
- quality is higher

The organizations that achieve high People Equity (high alignment, capabilities, and engagement) have a distinct advantage over their competitors. And the individuals who apply this concept to their lives also win, as we shall see shortly.

WHAT HAPPENS WHEN ACE IS LOW?

Another way to think about how ACE affects us is to consider what happens when ACE is low. Figure 2 summarizes the outcomes of low alignment, capabilities, and engagement. As you can see, low ACE leads to many dysfunctional consequences such as overstaffing, burnout, high rework, and low productivity.

ACE AND THE INDIVIDUAL

These aren't just corporate problems—they are individual concerns as well. People lose energy, stress levels send them over the edge, and they begin to unravel in both their work and home life. As you can see in figure 3, many individuals who are in situations with high conflict and low teamwork, face monotony or

FIGURE 2. The Impact of Low Alignment, Capabilities, and Engagement on Organizations

Low Alignment	Low Capabilities	Low Engagement
• many urgent but not important activities	• unable to meet customer requirements	• low productivity due to mediocre energy
• burnout or talent loss—working hard, but not smart	• high rework	• unmarketable employees retire in place
• overstaffing to compensate for time lost on low value activities	• overstaffing to meet standards or customer requirements	• low referrals of new talent from existing workforce
• low teamwork; high conflict across interdependent units	• employee/ supervisory burnout; turnover because of performance shortfalls with customers	• cynical or apathetic culture

Source: Adapted from W. Schiemann, *The ACE Advantage: How Smart Companies Unleash Talent for Optimal Performance*, 2012.

frustration due to more rework, deal with increased stress that can lead to burnout, or have low energy levels become apathetic or cynical. Those we have interviewed over the years describe coming home drained or overwrought, often leading to strained relationships with spouses or children. Some who can will leave the organization, but that can also create family and career disruptions. In short, low ACE hurts both the organization and the individual.

BIG BANG

But what happens when both the organization and the individual have high ACE? Bang! I know you have seen it. Individuals and

FIGURE 3. The Impact of Low Alignment, Capabilities, and Engagement on Individuals at Work

Low Alignment	Low Capabilities	Low Engagement
• lack of clear plan and prioritized actions	• unable to meet my stakeholders' (e.g., spouse, children, boss, friends) expectations	• low energy, apathetic or cynical
• burnout—working hard, but not smart	• unmarketable	• low productivity or accomplishments
• overspending personal time on low or no value activities	• not having the skills to be successful at things you value	• fuzzy or limited career or life path
• high conflict with others	• limited support network	• lack of clear values to guide priorities

teams thrive; the company, association, agency, or department often exceeds its goals; and there is a wonderful feeling of accomplishment and fulfillment. Based on our case studies, focus groups, and interviews with hundreds of people, we believe that high ACE is a win-win for the organization and the individual. Most of us have experienced that wonderful moment at work when we or someone around us is revved. The same can be said for other aspects of one's life when these features are in sync with a person's relationships, religion, or hobbies.

While both individuals and organizations thrive when ACE is high, other players are important in creating an environment where that can happen—that is, they are enablers that allow this Big Bang to occur. Human resources professionals, senior leaders, and immediate managers can play a major role in creating these types of environments. For example, has the organization actively hired people who will feel energized in their culture? Do senior leaders provide a compelling vision of the future? Does the immediate manager value individual differences and leverage each person to his or her best strengths? The same can be said of relationships: Do your relation-ships energize or deplete you?

The remainder of this part includes three chapters on align-ment, capabilities, and engagement in both a work and a nonwork context, so you can begin to see how you can create high ACE for yourself and for others.

3

Alignment

*I find that I am most happy and healthy when I am living
in alignment with my goals, dreams, and principles.*

—Dr. Steve Maraboli, *Unapologetically You:
Reflections on Life and the Human Experience*

When I was driving on a dusty road to Tijuana many moons ago,
alignment was the first word that popped into my head. The road—
when it could be called a road—was full of huge, car-swallowing pot-
holes before entering Tijuana. At the end of this road were many auto
repair shops waiting for their prey—wobbly wheeled drivers like me.
Back then, alignment was most often used to describe how well tires
on a car were calibrated to move in sync in order to minimize tire wear.
Today, the term is often used in a different context. Are a husband and
wife aligned about how to raise the kids? Are the kids aligned with
their parents' values or those of their church or synagogue? Is Congress
aligned with the president on how to raise revenue or cut expenses?

ALIGNMENT AT WORK

In the work context, as described before, alignment can be most
simply expressed as, "Are we all rowing in the same direction?" One
colleague described an episode when he was a camp counselor on

Lake Coeur d'Alene. "Two boys were in a canoe, which was spinning around in circles. Both were paddling furiously, but not balancing each other's strokes. Neither had a clue why they weren't making any progress."

This drives home the picture. Is the organization aligned with the expectations of its customers? Are the senior leaders aligned on the direction of the firm? Are departments aligned with the business strategy and priorities? Is your unit aligned with the goals of the department and the organization in general? Are you aligned with your colleagues in your values? Do you all believe, for example, that ethics or diversity is important or that customer service is a key principle?

When we move to the implications for you, the question becomes, are you aligned with the job and the organization, your relationships, your lifestyle (or life choices), and so forth? Or perhaps, stated a different way, are the job and organization aligned with your life goals and your values?

Let's start with your job first. Take the short quiz in figure 4, and let's see what you think. Simply choose the answer that is closest to your view.

Add the numbers you chose. A total score of 26 to 30 indicates that you are highly aligned in your work. Scores between 16 and 25 indicate that you are only partially aligned. Scores below 15 indicate a level of misalignment.

If you are fully aligned, congratulate yourself; you are among only 31 percent of workers. More than two-thirds of the rest of the workforce feels some level of misalignment. The challenge is to understand why you are not fully aligned. Take a moment to reflect on why you think you may or may not be aligned. Jot down a few ideas now regarding your level of alignment and what may be causing it.

Let's take a look at the drivers of alignment—the factors that cause low or high alignment. Some typical alignment drivers include:

- the level of alignment you see between what the organization promises to deliver to customers and what the organization actually delivers

FIGURE 4. How Aligned Are You at Work?

	Strongly Disagree	Disagree	Neutral	Agree	Strongly Agree
I am aligned with the overall goals and values of the organization.	1	2	3	4	5
I have clear, measurable performance goals.	1	2	3	4	5
I understand how what I do adds value to the organization and its customers.	1	2	3	4	5
My rewards (e.g., pay, recognition, autonomy) are closely connected to my performance.	1	2	3	4	5
Everyone here shares the same priorities.	1	2	3	4	5
My career goals are aligned with the opportunities offered by my employer.	1	2	3	4	5

TOTAL ALIGNMENT _____
Score (add up your score for the questions)

- your understanding of your organization's mission, strategy, and priorities
- your understanding of how your department fits into that plan
- the metrics that are used to evaluate the organization, the department, and your performance; the link between rewards and performance

At the personal level, alignment drivers include the process for setting your goals, the effectiveness of performance feedback you receive (and listen to), your understanding of what success looks like, and the link between success and your rewards. Figure 5 displays some of the typical alignment drivers.

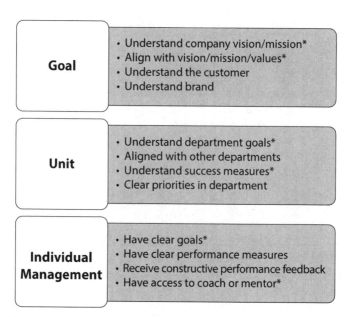

FIGURE 5. Typical Alignment Drivers

The next important question is this: Can you control or influence those drivers? If not, you may be in the wrong job, under the wrong boss, or in the wrong organization. To avoid prolonged misalignment and its negative consequences, consider how to create change. In the area of alignment, you most likely cannot change the level of alignment of the senior team or the direction of the company, but there are things you can do to enhance your alignment and thus reduce the stress of low alignment.

Taking Action

Figure 5 presents a list of many drivers of alignment at the organization, unit, and individual levels. The drivers that can be influenced most by the individual employee are marked with asterisks. For example, while you may not agree with the goals or direction of a company, you can certainly take steps to understand what the goals and direction are.

If you have too many drivers in your situation that are not controllable, it may be better to take a different career path or work for a different organization—if at all possible. The controllable drivers may be changed by asking for a new work assignment, getting with a different boss or group of peers, or discussing issues of performance or development candidly with your manager. Communication is key.

If you do not understand the organization's direction or how your job and the organization fit together, you can discuss this with your manager or perhaps with a third party. Often, there are other places you can go to read more about an organization's mission and goals. This requires being proactive and not waiting to be told.

Other major sources of stress and frustration include performance goals, performance reviews, and the alignment of your views of performance with the views of others. Some people we have interviewed find their performance goals unclear, or they don't see how they help the organization be successful. This can be a great conversation to have with your immediate manager. If that manager cannot answer those questions, start thinking about a move to a different unit.

Managers tell us that performance feedback is one of the most difficult things they do. They dread coming into a review meeting in which they will have to give negative feedback about someone's performance. And most employees don't make the process any easier. Most employees, the research says, come into a review with higher views of their performance than the reviewer. This certainly creates frustration. Psychologically, this can cause employees to shut down and not really listen to the full story or engage in a fruitful conversation. In many cases, both the manager and the subordinate dread the event.

However, some organizations have been able to reduce this stress by increasing the frequency of conversations throughout the year rather than having a major one-shot event. If your company does not give regular feedback, ask your manager to set up more frequent minireviews or directional feedback sessions. Some employees have communicated with their bosses throughout the year so that they don't have the bias of being influenced by what was done most recently. Or some employees send their managers some of their thoughts before the review, which helps the manager see an employee's viewpoint while preparing for the session. This also reduces situations where the manager feels locked into a position and the employee feels backed into a corner.

Another source of misalignment at work is compensation. A majority of people do not feel they are paid or rewarded enough. Welcome to the real world! To be fair, many managers we have interviewed wish that they had higher budgets to pay their employees more, and they often regret when employees are not recognized for their good work. While well meaning, managers can simply get overwhelmed in the course of their daily demands. But conversation can help, especially with recognition or other forms of reward. If your performance is high, a boss who wants to retain your talent will try to find other perks that are valuable to you.

Today, more organizations are asking their leaders to be flexible and to try to match rewards to the needs of different employees. For example, while your boss may not be able to give you the extra 2 percent raise you wanted, he or she may be able to give you other perks, such as a more flexible schedule or more autonomy in your work. Of course there are constraints, but there are negotiable elements in most situations. Don't be afraid to ask if you deserve the consideration.

The last major area of misalignment is values. In the movie *The Devil Wears Prada*, journalist Andrea Sachs is looking for work and eventually is hired to be the assistant of the very demanding Miranda Priestly, the editor of *Runway* magazine. However, Andrea does not have a strong alignment between her values and those of Miranda. In order to fit in and do well at her job, Andrea makes extreme changes that end up greatly affecting her work and private life. At the end, Andrea ends up leaving *Runway* magazine in order to pursue a job that is more aligned with her values.

While easier to see in a movie, many of us have been in situations in which it is clear that our values are not in sync with those of others or of the organization. While every incident should probably not be run all the way up the flagpole, a pattern of incidents should cause you to question how fulfilled you can be in a particular environment. Howard Winkler, former chair of the HR Certification Institute, said, "When making a tough decision, stick with your core values. You will be immensely happier afterwards."

Now, let's turn to nonwork life. In this segment on alignment as well as the upcoming discussions on capabilities and engagement, I have selected quizzes and examples primarily related to relationships, which was the primary nonwork area of fulfillment in most of our research.

ALIGNMENT IN NONWORK LIFE: RELATIONSHIP FULFILLMENT

Take a minute to complete the questions in figure 6 to determine your alignment with a friend, spouse, or family member (pick one). Choose the number for each question, from "Strongly Agree" to "Strongly Disagree," that best represents your feelings about that issue.

FIGURE 6. How Aligned Are You?

	Strongly Disagree	Disagree	Neutral	Agree	Strongly Agree
We have mutual agreed-upon expectations of our relationship.	1	2	3	4	5
We have discussed and agree on the goals or purpose of our relationship.	1	2	3	4	5
We both share similar values.	1	2	3	4	5
Our priorities are usually in sync.	1	2	3	4	5
We enjoy and share similar activities, friends, and hobbies.	1	2	3	4	5
We are rarely misaligned with each other.	1	2	3	4	5

TOTAL ALIGNMENT _____
Score (add up your score for the questions)

Add the numbers you chose. If you score 26 to 30, you are highly aligned. A score of 16 to 25 means that you are partially aligned. Scores below 15 suggest that you have a good deal of misalignment in your relationship.

If you are fully aligned, congratulations. If not, once again it is important to understand why. Are you surprised? What do you think is behind your level of alignment with someone with whom you have this relationship? You may want to jot down your thoughts while they are fresh on why your alignment is not as high as it could be.

Just as with work, there are drivers of alignment. Some typical drivers include the following:

- Expectation gaps: Do the expectations of the other person match what you expect of your own behavior? Are your expectations of the other person matched by their behavior? Expectations could include time spent together, mutual shared activities, or exclusivity of relationship, for example.
- Values consistency: Misaligned values often lead to conflicts. Are you a stickler for being on time when your partner is often fashionably late? Do you have different ethical standards? Do you share common values regarding spending?
- Common activities, hobbies, and interests: Sometimes relationships are built and stay strong around one particular hobby such as bowling or playing bridge. Take a look at activities, hobbies, professions, and shared interests; these may be clues to future alignment.
- Common goals: Sometimes common goals can be elusive. For example, most dating couples don't ask about their goals regarding having children on the first date. But if they haven't talked about it before getting married, it is a gap that will often come back to bite them.

Taking Action

Alignment can often be improved by addressing the controllable drivers. For example, if you are in a relationship over time, check to see if you have enough alignment on values, interests, and activities to hold the relationship together. Lakshmi enjoyed shopping, reading, quiet strolls on the beach, and taking in a play or opera. Her husband was a photo junkie, spending hours touring countries and taking pictures and then Photoshopping for what felt like eons to her. He hated opera and theater and most of all shopping. Over time, the rare moments they spent holding hands on a deserted beach were not enough to keep them together.

Are there misalignments that will break the deal? Consider this relationship: Don thought everything was going swimmingly; Kate thought otherwise as time progressed, and their relationship did not appear headed for marriage. Don asked her, "Why do I need to get married if we are having a good time?" Kate replied that she thought that people who really love each other would get married. Don had had cold feet before and didn't see why they should rush into something so important. Kate wanted to move faster and eventually broke it off. Don asked, "If we are 80 percent common spirits, how can we let the official act of getting married spoil everything?" It was clear that Kate had a different life goal, and marriage represented a key life stepping-stone—the ultimate contract and commitment.

Many of the alignment drivers can be enhanced by communication in your relationships or with a significant other early on. Conversations with outside coaches can also provide a balancing perspective. Good communication often brings out those perceived differences in a constructive conversation. Pretending that they don't exist can lead to disaster over time.

Can alignment be changed? Yes, it is possible. A special couple that I know met in one of the most misaligned situations. She was at a protest rally against the Vietnam War and he was a Young Republican supporting it. They met, they argued, and they fell in love. You might ask how that can happen with such diverging views. They shared so many other common interests in their lives that they overlooked their political differences. And over time, each of them was willing to listen to the viewpoints of the other, sometimes swaying their opinion—other times not. What was important was that they were both highly educated and respected the differences of political philosophy and their spouse's freedom to practice their own form of it. Another example is religion. Long-term couples who were brought up in different religions often tell a similar story—namely, that each spouse respected the differences in their religious beliefs and allowed their partner the freedom to express these differences.

SELF-ALIGNMENT

Despite jobs and relationships being the two most important areas of alignment for most people, internal self-alignment is critical. What do I mean by self-alignment? Think about your collection of values, goals, and actions. Sometimes your actions are not aligned with your espoused values or goals. For example, if you set a goal to lose fifteen pounds by summer, but your actions do not change, you will not meet that goal. If you fail to meet a goal that is important to you, you end up disappointed in yourself or depressed, and this detracts from your overall fulfillment. Or you might be working for a firm that you see undermining values that you and the organization itself claim to support. If you take no action to address this, you are then in a situation of personal misalignment between what you believe and your actions. This misalignment creates tension and reduces fulfillment. It is important to recognize these situations and to reduce internal misalignments as soon as possible, because those weigh on you both consciously and subconsciously.

I will come back to this issue in Part III of this book, where I discuss values, goals, and actions in much more depth.

4

Capabilities

Man often becomes what he believes himself to be. If I keep on saying to myself that I cannot do a certain thing, it is possible that I may end by really becoming incapable of doing it. On the contrary, if I have the belief that I can do it, I shall surely acquire the capacity to do it even if I may not have it at the beginning.

—Mahatma Gandhi

When I recently checked into a hotel in Aurangabad, India, I had a wonderful experience. I was greeted at my car by a manager, offered a passion fruit drink as I entered the lobby, and asked to sit for a moment to relax. He didn't launch into the usual "Let me check your reservation. May I have your credit card? Can you sign here?" Instead, he wanted to know how my journey was. Was I hungry? What were my plans? Only then did he begin to offer descriptions of how the hotel could serve me and counsel relative to the sites I wanted to visit. The staff then took me to my room to ensure it was satisfactory before I checked in to the hotel. This approach exceeded my expectations as a guest. I was not burdened with long waits and useless information. It was a perfect example of how a set of capabilities was tailored to my needs. They treated me as an individual and tried to make my experience fulfilling.

Our second key factor, capabilities, includes not only the skills or competencies of people but also their ability to bring the right information or resources to a situation. The individual is at the center of it all. As humans, it is important to feel competent. Much early psychological research, beginning with infants and young children, highlights this crucial psychological need. People, regardless of age, want and need to feel competent at whatever they do: raising children, performing their job or hobby, or playing a game. Children who fail at a game repeatedly avoid it in the future; it is too demotivating if you never win. The same is true at work. If you, or the unit in which you work, are low in capabilities, this spills over to your motivation and your focus over time.

While your view of your capabilities is important, we live in a world that judges the value of those capabilities. At work, it is a manager or an external or internal customer who judges the value of your work. In your personal life, there are many stakeholders—people that matter in your life: loved ones, family, teammates, colleagues on a community board, or hobbyist friends. Anyone who can influence your life is a stakeholder—or customer, if you will.

CAPABILITIES AT WORK

Thomas Friedman, the *New York Times* columnist and author of *The World is Flat*,[1] says that "being average is over," meaning that what was medium performance historically will no longer cut it in the new competitive world. The performance bar is being raised every day as competition from every side increases—coworkers or fellow students, new hires, and those offering similar services from other parts of the globe, whether physically or virtually, on the web. Friedman contends that those who have unique capabilities will have many job opportunities and earn a lot, while those who do not will have low job security and earn little.

Are you growing your capabilities so you have as many options as possible in the future? I recently interviewed a vice president of human resources who didn't start on the fast track. In fact, she started far from it. She was born the youngest of twelve children to a father who was a farmer and a mother who took odd sewing jobs to make money. She just hoped to be able to finish high school; college was out of the question. Her first job was working as a minion for a tax department, making copies or doing whatever else was needed. From there she launched into an administrative role, which set her on the path to becoming a junior HR person and ultimately a department manager. She attended night school for fifteen years to complete a college degree. After she jumped to a major HR role, she went back to get her MBA to ensure her ability to play in the boardroom.

Today she leads HR for a 1,200-employee bank. A strong vision, clear goals, and great attitude coupled with the willingness to develop the right skills enabled her to achieve career success—an integral part of her overall fulfillment.

Are you continuing to develop your capabilities? Take the short quiz in figure 7, and let's see what you think. As in the prior questionnaire, simply choose the answer that is closest to your view. Stakeholders include anyone who uses or evaluates your services or work output.

Add the numbers you chose. A score of 26 to 30 indicates that you have strong capabilities to deliver high value to your customers. Scores of 21 to 25 indicate that you have fairly good capabilities. A score of 16 to 20 indicates that there are some capabilities gaps. Scores below 15 indicate major capabilities gaps.

If you have strong capabilities, consider yourself fortunate and perhaps well prepared for next steps in your life plan. However, more than two-thirds of respondents will feel they have some capabilities gaps. Furthermore, you may want to compare your own judgment with the perceptions of others, as people tend to overestimate their own capabilities. One good exercise would be for you to pick three work stakeholders and ask them for feedback related to your capabilities. Use the questions in figure 7 as a guide. We have found this to be a helpful reality check. How does your self-perception compare with others? Are you surprised at your score? What areas might be holding your capabilities back?

FIGURE 7. How Effective Are Your Capabilities at Work?

	Strongly Disagree	Disagree	Neutral	Agree	Strongly Agree
I have the skills, knowledge, or experiences necessary to meet my customers' or stakeholders' expectations.	1	2	3	4	5
Customers or stakeholders would rate my quality of service (speed of response, ability to solve problems, anticipating their needs) as high.	1	2	3	4	5
I have the technical resources and tools I need to meet my customers' or stakeholders' expectations.	1	2	3	4	5
I have the information I need to meet my customers' or stakeholders' expectations.	1	2	3	4	5
Customers or stakeholders would rate my teamwork as excellent.	1	2	3	4	5
Customers, stakeholders, or those most knowledgeable about what I do would rate my capabilities as among the best of people who do that work.	1	2	3	4	5

TOTAL CAPABILITIES _____
Score (add up your score for the questions)

The value is in understanding why there are capabilities gaps. As we did with alignment, let's take a look at the drivers of capabilities—the factors that cause low or high capabilities. Some typical capability drivers include education, being a strong team player, having a good fit between your skills and the job requirements, being a good communicator, having clear expectations of what stake-holders or customers expect, having good measures of the value you deliver, being able to access the right information that you need to deliver value to customers and those around you, and having sufficient tools or resources that are needed to be successful in the job or in any task for that matter.

Figure 8 shows some of the typical capabilities drivers that can influence your capabilities score. The items with asterisks are typically more controllable by you.

The next important question is this: Which drivers can I control? To avoid prolonged capabilities gaps and their negative consequences, consider how to improve your capabilities. Although you cannot change the competencies of the senior team in your company or your boss, there are many things you can do to enhance your own capabilities, thereby reducing the negative outcome of feeling that you are not having an impact or that you are not competent.

If you have too many capabilities drivers that are not controllable, it may be best to seek a different job or consider an alternative

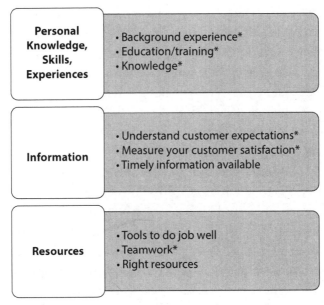

FIGURE 8. Typical Capabilities Drivers

career path. While that is not always possible, you can at least focus on areas where you have some degree of control. You can seek more training or discuss issues of performance or development candidly with your manager. If that doesn't work, and you are in a larger organization, you may want to talk to someone in human resources to discuss these issues and possibly transfer to another position.

Taking Action

The most basic driver of capabilities is having competencies to do tasks in your job well. Competencies include your knowledge, skills, experiences, and behaviors. Most of us have a self-perception of those competencies. However, it is important that others who depend on you or evaluate your contribution at work see these competencies in the same way that you do. As is frequently the case, we all have blind spots—areas where others see us differently than we see ourselves. It is important to get reality checks periodically to ensure that we are not out of touch with how the world views us. For example, are you noticed or recognized for your skills and related performance? Do people come to you for your knowledge or expertise? Does your background or experience provide you with valuable insights that you can use in your current tasks? Have you gotten candid feedback from your boss or peers on how well your skills stack up against those needed for your position?

Organizations that have 360-degree feedback—feedback from your boss, peers, and subordinates (where applicable)—are quite helpful from a development standpoint. If your organization does not do this, perhaps you can obtain informal feedback by reaching out to peers to ask questions like "If there was one area I could improve most, what would it be?" or "What do you think might be most beneficial from a career standpoint?" Answers to these questions move conversations from the past to the future. Then ask yourself this question: How can I grow and perform better?

One colleague questioned whether this can really be done for jobs that have less latitude. The short answer is that while some jobs have virtually no latitude, you can almost always do more than you originally think. I certainly did this earlier in my life in retail jobs, as a drill press operator, as a mechanic, and even as a batch assembly line employee. In hindsight, I probably asked too many questions or pushed too hard on the assembly line, leading to performance that was "too high," according to my supervisor. That was my first lesson in group norms; I got booted to a maintenance job, which had more flexibility, probably suiting me better at the time. I painted, did landscaping, and learned mechanical skills. I certainly didn't plan to spend a career in this role, but I sure know how to deal with a rusty pipe and manage landscaping challenges today.

In one job, when I asked how I could improve, one coworker said, "Who cares? You will be stuck in this job for the rest of your life and the boss won't change a thing." Despite having no other work at the time, I sucked it up for a short while, but immediately began looking for other working conditions where I would be treated with dignity. A key question that I use in my coaching work is, Will they ask for *you*?

At the end of the day, you bring one critical element to your organization, and that's your unique talent. In other words, you bring a set of experiences, know-how, skills, and behaviors to your organization. The question is, then, whether those skills are valued at the level they need to be for you to feel fulfilled and for the organization to feel it is getting good return on its investment in you.

Value is in the eyes of the beholder, and for you to control your own future, you must offer value to others. To understand that value, customer or stakeholder feedback is important. Most of us deliver something to someone. Our deliverables can be products or services. As organizations have learned through much research, customers can make or break your business. Internal departments also have internal customers or, as they often prefer to call them, stakeholders. As mentioned earlier, stakeholders include any person or group who can influence your success or the success of your unit or organization. When stakeholders view your individual or department work output as having high value, they are supportive. Highly rated departments often have higher budgets, more staff, and more influence than those that are rated low in value. When stakeholders see low value, they withhold support and can even sabotage your success. It is important to know how these stakeholders see your work and the work of your organization.

Ideally, your organization uses surveys, focus groups, interviews, or other assessment tools to gain feedback from stakeholders, providing you with important feedback on how they see value. But even if you do not have this type of formal feedback, you can engage your stakeholders in conversations. Do stakeholders feel there is high value in what you and your unit deliver? Do they frequently thank you for what you do? Would they prefer that your function was outsourced?

Find out what would be the most important thing you could improve. These are important self-awareness questions about your performance and the competencies that support your performance. If your capabilities are low or insufficient and you do not feel confident about or recognized for your mastery, you can take actions to improve those skills or experiences. Talk to your manager, mentor, or someone in HR about ways to grow your skills; most organizations would prefer to retain motivated and aligned employees if they are willing to upgrade their skills. The first step is being honest with yourself about your capabilities and then seeking support.

You may be surprised how many people will offer to help you improve your skills or knowledge. In some cases, it may be time to go back to school or take advantage of external programs. But there are low-cost options as well, such as rotational assignments, participating in local professional organizations, or asking to be assigned to different types of projects. In the next section of this book, I will talk about career paths in more depth.

Training is often an area to consider. Emilio, a fast-food employee whom I interviewed years ago, told me that he was ashamed and embarrassed when customers would get angry or frustrated with him for not doing something right. He went on to say that he had never been trained on the register and had problems placing the correct orders and making adjustments when orders were changed. The same went for his fries. While he finally got the hang of it, he had never been trained on the fryer and was embarrassed when people sent back under- or overcooked fries. Having satisfied customers is more than asking with a big smile, "Do you want fries with that?"

Another worker at a global pizza chain shared that she lasted merely four days on the job. Why only four days? Here's her story:

> I did not feel I was trained enough to fulfill my job tasks. I did not possess the right capabilities to do what was required of me. For example, I did not receive training on waitressing nor did I know anything about the menu. It was my first days and the restaurant was so busy. I was tossed in as a waitress to fill the gap and be able to serve the customers in a timely manner. However, I was so focused on being able to do things right that I did not focus on other tasks. I spilled a soda on a customer and burned the breadsticks! Overall, at the time I did not have the capabilities necessary to successfully perform at the restaurant and that caused me to dread going to work, and I quit after only four days.

In both of these cases, poor training was a culprit, leading to negative outcomes. If your organization has training that will help you succeed, you need to be proactive to find a way to access it.

Another major driver of strong capabilities is teamwork. Most organizations today—sports teams, employers, volunteer organizations, hobby groups—are looking for team players. If you are a lone wolf, you need to seek the small set of professions in which you can do your individualist thing. But even if your current role doesn't require huge amounts of teamwork, the odds are that you will be called upon to develop good teamwork skills during your lifetime. While most people only remember heroes' names—such as Neil Armstrong (first man on the moon), Jeff Gordon (champion racer), Juliet Gordon Lowe (founder of the Girl Scouts), Mahatma Gandhi (great leader of Indian independence)—most heroes became heroes because of a well-functioning team behind them. If you need development in this area, take a teamwork course, join a group in which you are a member of the team rather than the leader, or ask for coaching from other team members.

The last major driver of capabilities is information and resources. If you are short on either, it is important to discuss these issues with your manager, work coach, or other leaders. Help them see how the shortfall is affecting key stakeholders or customers. Learn to be a lobbyist. Author and speaker Daniel Pink reminds us that we are all in "sales." Even if we don't sell products for our organizations, we sell our ideas and need to influence others to be successful.[2] He argues that one of the most important things each of us does is sell ourselves—our reputation, capabilities, engagement, or ideas. Our level of success in selling ourselves affects the level of influence we have on our work, friends, or community. It affects the type of performance rating we get and the types of opportunities that are offered to us, and it determines whether our ideas are adopted by others.

Being an effective lobbyist is a key life lesson. You need to become a good communicator no matter what you do in life, unless your goal is to become a hermit. It is only through strong communication that we influence others, lobby for resources, give and receive actionable feedback, and arrive at common ground with peers, other departments, and key stakeholders. If your communication skills are weak, chasing another job won't help you in the long run. It is better to dig in now and begin doing things that will enhance your capabilities. For example, you could take a writing class or sign up for a public speaking course. Volunteer to speak in public, even if it terrifies you. I did that much earlier in my career, enabling me to pursue several professions, volunteer activities, and hobbies that depend on some amount of public speaking or good communication skills. Once you do it, you will look back on it fondly.

Another idea is to take an acting class, even if you aren't planning to become an actor. Such courses teach you how to improvise, think on your feet, react to others in productive ways, and improve your communication agility. This is also an excellent area in which to use a coach or mentor who will provide candid feedback and give you new insights about how your communications are received by others.

CAPABILITIES IN NONWORK LIFE: RELATIONSHIP MANAGEMENT

Once again, the examples in nonwork life focus on relationships, which the majority of people rate as the most important nonwork area of fulfillment in their lives. Take a minute to complete the questions in figure 9 to determine your capabilities with friends, your spouse, or a family member (pick one). Choose the number for each question, from "Strongly Agree" to "Strongly Disagree," that best represents your feelings about that issue.

FIGURE 9. How Effective Are Your Capabilities in Your Nonwork Life?

	Strongly Disagree	Disagree	Neutral	Agree	Strongly Agree
I have the right education to connect with or be accepted by those with whom I wish to interact.	1	2	3	4	5
I have values that others respect.	1	2	3	4	5
I am often sought out by others for my knowledge, skills, or expertise.	1	2	3	4	5
My physical appearance commands attention to others in a way that matches the image I wish to project.	1	2	3	4	5
Others have told me that I bring unique value to a situation or relationship.	1	2	3	4	5
I am often relied upon because of my access to information or the right resources.	1	2	3	4	5

TOTAL CAPABILITIES _____
Score (add up your score for the questions)

Add the numbers you chose. If you score 26 to 30, you have relatively high capabilities in your relationships. A score of 16 to 25 means that you have moderate capabilities but some gaps. Scores below 15 suggest that you have significant capabilities gaps in your relationships.

If you are highly capable with relationships, congratulations. As I suggested earlier, go to two or three people with whom you have a relationship and ask for feedback related to the questions in figure 9. Do you receive the same scores? If not, or if the scores are low, it is important to understand why. Jot down your initial thoughts on why your score is as it is. What are your capabilities strengths when it comes to a relationship? What are your weaknesses? Are there any capabilities that have sunk relationships in the past?

_____

_____

_____

_____

_____

Taking Action

Just as with work, there are drivers of relationship capabilities. Some typical capabilities drivers include these:

- Education: Does your significant other or partner value your academic experience? I'm sure we can all find an example of a relationship where educational levels are different. PhDs don't always marry PhDs. Much depends on fit and respect. Some people we interviewed felt that it was important for their partner to have a similar educational background so that they would have compatibility across mutual friends.

- Lifestyles: Most relationships thrive when there are complementary lifestyles. Check your friends for this one. Early risers are often married to a late-night partner. This may be convenient when raising children, caring for pets, or covering the broad spectrum of daily needs. Rarely do both partners equally love house painting, auto repairs, decorating, furniture refinishing, or a myriad of other things that keep a household together. Ideally, their strengths complement each other.
- Teamwork: Regardless of whether it is a team of two in a budding relationship or individual members of a larger group, most people value others they can count on to support the team. Can one partner count on the other to pick up the kids on time? Can one gamer count on another to be there for a cool new game? Does your softball league count on you to be great at getting on base?
- Access to resources: Capabilities are often judged not only by what someone brings in their education or experience but by the resources that are attached to them. Will a potential spouse have sufficient financial resources to make the relationship viable economically? Do your friends like to hang out with you because of the network you have on Facebook? Many new businesses have started up because one person had the marketing savvy (think Steve Jobs of Apple) and the other had the technical know-how (think Steve Wozniak of Apple). Jobs made it a point to have connections to the design and money world, while Wozniak had great resources in the techie space.

Capabilities can often be improved by addressing the controllable drivers. For example, if you are in a relationship with someone who is counting on you to complete your degree, you can control that. If a team is counting on you to put together a new website for them, you have the skills to do that. When it comes to learned skills and knowledge, you have a good deal more control than you do regarding capabilities related to natural ability areas—body size and shape, mental acumen, or spatial perception, for example.

At this time, you may not have much control over some areas. For example, one friend of mine devoted her early life to gaining advanced degrees in philosophy. She is more knowledgeable than most in this space, but it doesn't pay a lot. Her spouse was okay with that and did not enter the relationship counting on a lot of income from her career. But if she had been dating someone who was counting on a six-figure salary from her, in all likelihood the relationship would have degraded. Another couple in my town owns a bike shop. They both value someone who has the physical capabilities to go on long bike rides with biking groups. If one partner simply didn't have the physical stamina or coordination to do that, they might have had a compromised relationship.

As it turns out, communication is key once again! Many of the capabilities drivers can be enhanced by communicating with your significant other or group early on. A good coach may be able to help you identify skills and knowledge areas that will be important for your career or help you achieve broader life goals.

5

Engagement

The energy of the mind is the essence of life.

—Aristotle

WHY ENGAGEMENT IS GOOD FOR YOU AND YOUR ORGANIZATION

Think about a time when you were really energized or revved about something in your work or personal life. The odds are that you put in all the effort needed and more. You may have been excited to take on additional duties and help others involved achieve the same level of success and enthusiasm. That energy is what I mean by engagement, and it leads to positivity in all aspects of life.

My friend Mike was a model railroad enthusiast. He also loved his job as a programmer and often worked well past business hours. But after working, he would stay up into the wee hours of the night putting new track in his train line. In the morning, Mike was a bit tired, yes, but happy—I might even say contented and energized—because he had made progress on his model railroad plan. For Mike, it wasn't work or a hobby—it was both. He found ways to balance his energies across both parts of his life. Or, as one person at DonorsChoose.org expressed it on their website, "100% employer-paid benefits and 25 vacation days! Who doesn't love a company that values your health and wellness and encourages you to have a life outside of work? My outside interests make me a more creative and diverse employee, and that's valued here."[1]

Psychologists and physiologists tell us that this is not surprising. Engagement and enthusiasm have a positive effect on our brain chemistry and our moods and attitude. Our brains are more stimulated, secreting positive hormones—the opposite of when we feel frightened or threatened. When you achieve that "high," the odds are that you have high satisfaction. That may be because you have a satisfying boss with whom you share mutual commitments—he or she can count on you to do what it takes for the unit to be successful, and you can count on the boss to support you and help you be successful. Often, there is a strong feeling of mutual commitment to your colleagues and perhaps the organization. When you are really revved, you speak positively about the organization because you are proud to be a part of it.

We know that stress and dissatisfaction cause a negative cycle of brain and hormonal activity, which can lead to low energy, malaise, and even depression. Tom, a package goods delivery person, said, "I dread getting up on Monday morning. I just don't get excited about coming in to work." He is not alone. Many people feel this way. During the last recession, Gallup found that 18 percent of employees felt actively disengaged and 49 percent were disengaged.[2] Aon-Hewitt found that only 62 percent of employees were engaged worldwide.[3] Every day, many are saying "why bother?" in their work environment.

Being engaged in your work or personal life is a good thing for you, your employer, and your friends and family. Beyond work, it can mean being excited to put in more time or effort into relationships, hobbies, religion, or other activities. Just as with work, when you are engaged, you volunteer to do things rather than do them out of obligation.

Now here is a critical point: Engagement is not the responsibility of your work situation, your boss, your spouse, your parents, or your teacher. While those individuals may help or hinder engagement, it is up to *you* to determine if you are engaged or disengaged today and what you want to do about it.

ENGAGEMENT AT WORK

Take a minute to complete the questions in figure 10 to determine your engagement at work. Later, we will apply similar questions to other aspects of your life. Choose the number for each statement, from "Strongly Agree" to "Strongly Disagree," that best represents your feelings about that issue.

Add the numbers you chose. If you score 26 to 30, you are strongly engaged. A score of 16 to 25 means that you are partially engaged. Scores below 15 suggest that you have a good deal of disengagement in your work situation.

If you are strongly engaged, congratulate yourself; you are among only one-third of workers who feel that way today. Again, jot down

FIGURE 10. How Engaged Are You in Your Work Life?

	Strongly Disagree	Disagree	Neutral	Agree	Strongly Agree
Considering everything, I would rate my work life as excellent.	1	2	3	4	5
I am always willing to put in extra effort when needed.	1	2	3	4	5
I feel high energy and excitement when I am working.	1	2	3	4	5
I would recommend my workplace to a friend or colleague as a good place to work.	1	2	3	4	5
I am proud to tell people what I do for work.	1	2	3	4	5
I can trust people I work with, including my manager.	1	2	3	4	5

TOTAL ENGAGEMENT _____
Score (add up your score for the questions)

your thoughts on your current engagement level. Ask yourself why you feel this way. What do you think are the causes?

_____

_____

_____

_____

_____

If you are not fully engaged, it is important to understand why. To do that, we look to something we call drivers of engagement. Some typical engagement drivers include your supervisor or boss, your pay and benefits, how fairly you feel you are treated, whether you feel recognized for good work, your communication practices, your growth and development opportunities, your feelings of job security, support from your boss and peers, your comfort with the values or operating style of the organization, and your working conditions.

Take a minute to think about each of the factors listed in figure 11. Identify the ones that you feel are important but that represent a gap in your expectations. Note the two or three most important ones.

Taking Action

The next important question is this: Can you control or influence the engagement drivers? If not, you may be in the wrong job, working for the wrong boss, or with the wrong organization. To avoid prolonged disengagement and its negative consequences, consider a change. Perhaps it is only your boss and not the organization. In that case, you may be able to get transferred to another unit. If you really don't like the work, consider changing your job. If you disagree with

FIGURE 11. Engagement Factors

the values or the operating style of the organization, it may be time to look for a new company to work for if you can.

On the other hand, we have found that low engagement can often be improved by addressing the controllable drivers. For example, if you are not being recognized for good work, you can ask yourself whether you are indeed doing work worth recognizing. If not, perhaps it is time to step up. If you are, it may be helpful to talk to your boss or a coach about why you are not recognized for your contributions. Managers often are unaware that they are not providing recognition or take long-term performance for granted. A conversation can often alert them to the importance of your feeling that your work is valued.

The factors in figure 11 that are most controllable by you are marked with asterisks. For example, if you do not believe in the values or mission of the organization, you should find another company; disagreements over values or direction will continue to haunt you, and unless you are the founder or president of an organization, it is unlikely that you are going to change them. Pride in your work accomplishments is also an area that you control. Only you can be proud (or not) of the work you do. For example, Mack had a seven-to-four job that required mechanical work. Mack always talked about doing his work well. Others in the organization could count on Mack for high-quality output. He beamed when he talked about the work he did. He used to say, "Love what you do, and do what you love!" And I can tell you, it was contagious talking to Mack. He indirectly caused me to eventually move from a job that I didn't love to one that I did.

Although some marked areas in figure 11 may not be totally controllable by you, they are certainly open to influence by you. For example, if you are being treated with disrespect, you need to step up and discuss that with those who are offending you; you may be surprised at how a boss or a peer can change if they realize how much you are offended. Likewise, if expectations are unclear, you can sit down with your manager or coach to discuss them. Even pay and benefits for some jobs can be influenced by you; if you don't think you have been considered for a raise or are being paid less than other similar employees, you need to take action and at least have a conversation with your manager, HR rep, or an ombudsman if you are not being heard. Most people have far more influence than they realize.

If you have too many drivers that are not controllable, consider if the root cause of your dissatisfaction is career choice or organization. If you don't like the work, then it is usually more valuable to rethink your career and the type of job you do. While some people may be trapped in difficult circumstances, it is important to recognize that our minds are often our own worst enemy, locking us into patterns of thought based on what we have done in the past or what others around us are doing or have done. I will address this to a much greater extent in the next section of this book on career planning.

If you like doing the work, it is more likely the context that needs to be addressed. Look first to see if you have controllable engagement drivers by asking for a new work assignment, moving to a different boss or group of peers, or discussing issues of unfairness or perhaps disrespect. Communication is essential. Many of the engagement drivers can be enhanced by communication with your boss, your peers, or perhaps someone in human resources. Conversation with outside coaches—family, friends, a mentor, or a professional coach—can also provide a balanced perspective. However, here is a note of caution: If you spend time with people who are disengaged, cynical, and mistrusting, then all of their coaching will lead you down a doomed path to perennial unhappiness. On the other hand, if you hang out with people who are engaged, they can act as realistic role models and provide good counsel.

ENGAGEMENT IN NONWORK LIFE

Take a minute to complete the questions in figure 12 to determine your engagement with a friend, partner, or family member. Pick one person to think about as you answer the questions. Choose the number for each question, from "Strongly Agree" to "Strongly Disagree," that best represents your feelings about that issue.

Add the numbers you chose. If you score 26 to 30, you are strongly engaged. A score of 16 to 25 means that you are partially engaged. Scores below 15 suggest that you have a good deal of disengagement in your relationship.

If you are fully engaged, congratulations. If not, once again it is important to understand why. Jot down your thoughts on why your relationship may be more or less engaging. What do you think are the causes of the results you are getting?

Just as with work, there are drivers of relationship engagement. Some typical drivers include the behaviors of the other person, how fairly you feel you are treated, whether you feel recognized for things you do, the way you are communicated with, your agreement on values, and whether you feel that you are growing in the relationship.

FIGURE 12. How Engaged Are You in Your Relationship?

	Strongly Disagree	Disagree	Neutral	Agree	Strongly Agree
Considering everything, I would rate this relationship as excellent.	1	2	3	4	5
I am always willing to put in extra effort to support this relationship.	1	2	3	4	5
When around this person, I feel high energy and excitement.	1	2	3	4	5
I would recommend this person to other friends or colleagues.	1	2	3	4	5
I am proud to be associated with this person.	1	2	3	4	5
I can trust this person.	1	2	3	4	5

TOTAL ENGAGEMENT _____
Score (add up your score for the questions)

If you are not fully engaged, take a minute to think about each of the factors listed here and in figure 13. Identify the ones that are the most important to you and which ones have gaps from your expectations.

Taking Action

As with work, you have control over many of these engagement drivers. If not, you may be in the wrong relationship. To avoid prolonged disengagement and its negative effects, consider changing the nature of the relationship. We have all witnessed someone we know who has been in a relationship that is clearly not working. Often, they cannot see it themselves or they have become a "boiled frog." There is an adage that if a frog is tossed into boiling water,

FIGURE 13. Sample Relationship Drivers

- growing or learning in the relationship
- receiving support from the other person
- feeling recognized or appreciated for things you do
- feeling fairly treated
- having respectful communication
- being able to count on this person to do what they say they will do
- feeling proud to be associated with this person

it will jump out instantly, but if the water temperature increases slowly over time, the frog will continue to stay until it is way past medium rare. Many of us have seen people we know who are close to parboiled in certain relationships.

Low engagement can often be improved by addressing the controllable drivers. For example, if you are not being recognized for your contributions, discuss the issue and see what the other person in the relationship thinks about it. Perhaps others don't realize they are not acknowledging you. If they don't care, then you have to make choices. A conversation can often alert them to the importance of your feeling that you are valued. Or if you became involved with an individual for certain reasons—sex, fame, brain power—that are now not holding a full relationship together, then it is time to assess whether you can either improve or change the relationship.

Individual growth rates are often a key issue in flagging relationships. It may be that one partner is growing while the other is stalled or that one person is growing in a different direction. This is exacerbated by those who have formed relationships quickly or at early ages. Earlier in the book we discussed Carol and Victor, who married quite young. She was initially impressed with her clever and talented husband and his family—brothers and sisters with professional jobs and a family shore house. He was impressed with her intelligence and her homemaking (she was the Martha Stewart of her neighborhood). However, as each of them evolved, they grew in different directions. He was missing a fun side of his life, and she was missing a career that she could be proud of and that would give her fulfillment. Ultimately they separated, but not before they were nearly boiled frogs. When you are in a relationship, it is hard to objectively evaluate it. You have things that historically worked for you, but perhaps they no longer do, yet you keep hoping they will in the future. Rarely do people go back to what they were in the past. When this is happening, you need all the help you can get from trusted advisors such as friends, parents, mentors, and counselors. The first step to change is recognizing the gap.

In any relationship, communication is vitally important. Yet many of our interviewees talked about "shutting down" or avoiding difficult conversations. Some described worrying about hearing the wrong answer from a spouse, child, or friend. But most came back to communication as one of the key aspects of addressing the drivers of engagement in their relationships. More than half talked about the importance of conversations with outside sources—a coach, mentor, or even a psychologist—to help them obtain a more balanced view or confirm what they feared but had been denying.

Communication is not just about discovering the worst but about building stronger relationships through active listening, asking good questions, and sharing thoughts and feelings. Many relationships could be greatly enhanced by good self-assessment coupled with strong communication.

WHAT ABOUT BRIDGET?

In Part I of this book, we introduced Bridget, who was struggling with her career decisions and, in fact, with her life direction. She had had full-time jobs in retail and as an administrative assistant before returning to school to study psychology, but that was not very fulfilling. When she took the ACE challenge for both career and relationships, she scored low on alignment in her retail job but high on alignment in her administrative role with a small consulting firm. Her values were aligned with the firm's innovative focus, she received clear goals and direction, and she got rewarded for high performance.

For the retail job, she was overqualified, but for the consulting firm, she would be underqualified to continue beyond an administrative role. Her boss thought she had the aptitude for a more technical role with some sound psychological training. She scored low on engagement for the retail job—she had no passion for it— but she scored high for the consulting firm role, even though she was not fully qualified for some of the roles she got to observe. She felt energized by the environment, the interaction with clients, and the opportunity to make a difference that the firm espoused in its philosophy. But as she faced the end of her psychology training, she was torn about her next steps. Should she jump back to the consulting firm in a new role? Should she look for a corporate job? Which roles would help her balance her life with an impending marriage to someone who would be traveling a good deal? Also, she weighed how this decision would affect her having children and continuing her community service work, which was easy to do when she was in retail and in school.

She was not alone in these difficult decisions. The next sections of this book will provide guidance on how to approach similar situations. The choices and tradeoffs confronting Bridget are typical of those most of us face early on in our careers.

In this part of the book, you have learned about the importance of ACE as a tool for thinking about how you leverage value for organizations and groups that you interact with as well as for yourself. We all want to be aligned with something, feel competent, and be engaged in what we do. In the next part, I will turn to the "science" of becoming fulfilled and provide proven steps and tools to move from where you are today to a more fulfilled life.

PART III

THE SCIENCE OF FULFILLMENT

Truly believe in your abilities to shape
the world in which you live.
—Lance Miyamoto, chief human resources officer, Catalent

This part of the book will discuss the science of fulfillment. If you're not a scientific person, don't be frightened. A few of my reviewers were surprised by the word *science* in a book about fulfillment, but there has been a good deal of research into areas related to fulfillment, such as satisfaction, success, and happiness. Research can help us eliminate some things in our lives that clearly reduce fulfillment; it can also provide guidance into other actions that have been shown to help create a fulfilling and happy life.

First, in preparing for this book, the Metrus Institute interviewed more than one hundred people and surveyed far more across generations to identify the elements that seem to be important in achieving fulfillment. From our review of scientific studies, and from the numerous interviews we have conducted for this book, we have determined that *there are some clear guiding principles that are related to fulfillment*. Second, we can observe what people around us are doing every day—people working as generalists or specialists, people who are married or single, people who are workaholics or not, people with children or no children, people who work full time or part time, people who work for a large company or as entrepreneurs. If we become better observers of others, we can learn from what they have experienced and try to test or apply these lessons in our own lives. Part of the challenge for each of us is to determine which lessons are most helpful to us given our personalities and where we are on life's path. So what have we learned? Work and career were the driving force for life fulfillment for the vast majority of our interviewees and questionnaire respondents. This is true of baby boomers, Gen Xers, millennials—in essence, almost everyone we talked to.

As exemplified in a comment by Coretha Rushing, chief human resources officer at Equifax, "I don't believe you can separate work and non-work—today, they are so intertwined for most people." She worked her way up with early career successes at IBM, Pizza Hut (a division of Pepsi), and later at Coca-Cola before joining Equifax. She talked about the interplay of work, family, church, and other interests as part of a collage of factors in life fulfillment. For most people, a career clearly occupies a huge amount of their nonsleeping life.

Next, after work, relationships dominate conversations about fulfillment. Career and relationships are the two primary areas of fulfillment for most people. Because of this, work and career will be a centerpiece of examples shared in this section, with additional examples focused on relationships. Once you have seen the science applied to career and perhaps one other area of life, you should be able to then apply that thinking to any area of your life.

SOME GUIDING PRINCIPLES

The following are some guiding elements for creating life fulfillment that will be discussed in this section of the book:

- Creating clear life goals: Where would you like to be at the end of your life and how would you like to be remembered? What is your legacy?

- Identifying your drivers of fulfillment: What are the things that lead to high versus low fulfillment?
- Applying the ACE (alignment, capabilities, and engagement): How will you apply the principles that you learned about in Part II to help you understand and manage your drivers of life fulfillment?
- Creating your life map: How should you create a visual representation of how your life goals connect to where you are today, so that you can plan and invest your future time wisely?
- Building a personal scorecard: How can it help you measure your progress toward your life goals?
- Assessing yourself: How do you take an honest assessment of where you are today to set priorities for tomorrow?
- Creating a game plan for executing your life strategy: What actions will get you where you want to go?
- Tracking your progress: How well are you achieving your goals now, so you can make course corrections along the way?

In Part IV of this book, I will provide more on the art of fulfillment. What do more fulfilled people recommend after you have applied the science to navigate the rough waters that most of us will face at one time or another? How have they overcome setbacks? What are their core insights to getting and staying fulfilled? What are the key pieces of wisdom they want to pass along to you?

Note: many of the tools and worksheets in this section can be accessed at http://www.wschiemann.com/fulfilled.

6

Life Goals and Values

If You Don't Know Where You're Going, You'll
Probably End Up Somewhere Else
—book by Dr. David P. Campbell

The track-and-field pro, Carl Lewis, competed in four Olympic Games and won a total of nine gold Olympic medals. But it didn't happen overnight; he had been working on his track-and-field skills for many years, which ultimately allowed him to reach Olympic success.[1] Missy Franklin won a total of four gold medals at the 2012 Olympics in England in swimming. She had been an achiever since she learned how to swim as a young girl.[2]

When Michael Phelps, the Olympian with the most medals ever (twenty-two, including eighteen golds after the 2012 London Olympics), was interviewed after winning his final gold medal at those games, he said that he had always had a plan, and thus far he had fulfilled it on his way to Olympic gold. Wow! That's quite a statement, but when you look at the statements of most Olympic athletes, you'll find similar stories: clear goals, clear strategies, lots of training, focus, hitting the numbers, and a bit of luck in the end. In this chapter I will focus on the beginning of a journey to fulfillment—having clear goals. However, some Olympians have struggled with other aspects of their lives, including Phelps, who has racked up two DUI charges and gone through rehab for drug issues. As of this writing, he was back in training to make another competitive run at medals in 2016. He says he now has a better perspective, explaining, "The goals that I have are very lofty. I come into work with a purpose every day."[3]

Swimmer Ian Thorpe, the winningest Australian Olympic athlete of all time, has struggled with alcohol abuse and depression. Another silver medalist swimmer, Scott Miller, was arrested for drug possession. He told Australian media, "I've failed miserably," since his swimming career ended. Another silver medalist, skier Jeret "Speedy" Peterson, struggled with alcohol and drug abuse and committed suicide after his Olympic career ended.[4]

In China, many athletes cannot find jobs after their award-winning Olympic careers; some have even sold their gold medals. Perhaps these examples taken from the sports headlines point to the problem of having great short-term goals but not life-fulfilling long-term goals. It may be even worse for silver medalists because they may feel they missed the big award and had no other goals to head toward.[5]

VALUES: THE ULTIMATE ARBITER

All of us are driven by a set of values—what we believe is important in life. Do you believe in acting ethically? Is fairness important, and if so, what does that mean to you? Do you believe in sharing with others or in rugged individualism—only the strong survive? Are you spiritual? Are you conservative or liberal? What is the code of behavior that you endorse?

Successful organizations know that values are essential to success and that values differ among competitors. Dave Daley, the proprietor of Repairs Unlimited, an auto repair shop in New Jersey, telegraphs his values to his customers: honesty and integrity, open communication, and a fair deal. Because these are values that I can identify with as a customer, I have returned to Dave's shop for thirty-five years.

When I first went to Dave's place, he was apprenticing with his dad. It was clear that his father was fair with customers and was a straight shooter. He would go the extra mile to satisfy his customers. Their shop was not the cheapest, but for me they were the best value for the money. Dave learned his values at an early age and continued to stick to them after he took over the shop.

Dave's values are not confined to his work. He is also a family man, and while it is hard to find time when you are an entrepreneur, often working six days a week, he has managed to devote time to his family, learn scuba diving with his daughter, and get away for quality time together whenever possible.

We have all seen values go amok. The Enron scandal in the early part of this millennium was a case of ethics gone awry. Among other notorious failings, Enron's CEO and CFO reported information that was blatantly false, ruining the lives of many investors and employees in the process. Perhaps needless to say, those behaviors violated the publicly claimed values of the company.

Bernie Madoff is an example of someone who "made off" with other people's money, failing to operate in a manner that his investors had expected. He promised great financial returns for those who invested with him but could only sustain those returns as long as he brought in new investors.

Garry Ridge, the CEO of WD-40 Company (you probably have a can of his product to rid yourself of squeaks in your house), is a strong proponent of values. The organization has a set of six values that are the cornerstone of how they expect people to act. If you can't support those values, they tell you that WD-40 Company is the wrong place for you. Having strong values eliminates the need for lots of rules and policies. The simple question to any employee at WD-40 Company is this: Did you behave consistently with these values?

Their values also transcend different parts of the globe. Garry sent out a values challenge a few years ago and asked employees around the globe to make videos of how they live these values. The videos were amazing, with teams across the globe expressing unique ways of embodying WD-40 Company's values in their country.

This example is one of many that exemplify an important message: If you have strong values, then you don't need hundreds of rules in your life. The corollary for organizations is that they do not need hundreds of rules if they have strong values with which people are aligned.

Values are often shaped by early childhood experiences—baked in along the way. Consequently, values tend to endure throughout life and are difficult to change. Take Kerry and Kindra. They have three children and have inculcated them with strong values from early childhood. They have stressed things like sharing, not being self-centered, working hard, being spiritual, and respecting others. If you were to meet their kids, you would be constantly reminded that while they each have individual personalities, they all share some common values. As adults, they live those values in their careers and nonwork lives. All of them volunteer or coach others, they avoid actions and communications that disrespect others, and they all seem to be great team players. Their parents didn't need a lot of family rules. When the kids were teenagers, the values kept their hormones and behaviors in check.

WHAT ARE YOUR IMPORTANT LIFE VALUES?

Take a minute to think about your life values. Deep down, what do you hold near and dear? Is it fairness, ethical behavior, education, service to others, religious or spiritual values, or something else? If you are unsure, ask yourself what others do at times that makes you uncomfortable or upset. Are they violating some important value or principle that you believe in? What characteristics in others do you admire? If someone else were asked to describe five to seven characteristics about you, what would those be? Are they correct when you think about your inner self? In other words, is that the real you or a mask that you show others?

In this exercise, it is important to answer for the real you. Figure 14 has a place for you to list those values. For now, only complete the first column. A note of caution: if you are listing more

FIGURE 14. Life Values

Key Life Values	Behaviors That Exemplify Values	Behaviors That Violate Values

than seven values, you are probably not separating out the truly important ones. If you could only list five to seven key values, what would they be? The Ten Commandments that Moses brought down from Mount Sinai were later summarized this way: love God with all your heart, soul, and mind, and love your neighbor as yourself.[6] We want your equivalent of those top values.

If you are having trouble thinking of these, see the sidebar "Which Values Do You Hold Most Important?"

Which Values Do You Hold Most Important?

Here is a list of potential values that people often observe. Don't be limited by these values—this is just a starter list.

Which Values Do You Hold Most Important?

Risk Taking (high to low risk taker)

Communications Style (open/sharing or closed/personal)

Honesty (strict to loose interpretation)

Beliefs (conservative or liberal)

Teaming (high to low team affiliation)

Fairness (tighter or more relaxed)

Recognition (high to low need for recognition)

Spirituality (high to low)

Law and Rule Abiding (high to low)

Nurturing (high to low)

Ethics (strict to less strict standards)

Achievement (high, medium, low needs)

Respect (high to low)

Rewards (tangible like money or intangible like recognition or status)

Sociability (high to low)

Accountability (high to low)

Kindness (high to low)

Compassion (high to low)

To test the values you listed in figure 14, add some examples of your actions in the recent past that exemplify each value. The more specific you can be, the better, as it will help crystalize the meaning of the value.

Then, to understand what falls outside of your values, list one action that you have done in the past that violates that value. Be honest with yourself—we have all fallen from our ideals in the past, and it helps to understand clearly what that looks like.

Figure 15 has an example of a completed table.

FIGURE 15. Behaviors That Exemplify or Violate Life Values

Key Life Values	Behaviors That Exemplify Values	Behaviors That Violate Values
Fairness	At work I treat all people the same no matter what their ethnicity.	I sometimes make rude comments because of a person's background.
Respect	During arguments with friends, I try not to disrespect them in any way.	At times, I argue with others by insulting or putting them down.
A desire to advance myself	I try really hard to get good grades in school as well as seek opportunities to develop myself.	I say I want to get good grades, but I don't always do what it takes.
Responsibility	When I am being held accountable for something, I try my hardest to get it done, as I know others are counting on me.	At times, I fall short on my responsibilities, sometimes letting others down.
Caring for others	I enjoy being able to show others that they are appreciated.	I can be cold and uncaring when I don't like another person.

With a good values foundation, it is time to turn to life goals. Later you will test yourself to ensure that your life goals and life values are in sync.

WHAT ARE LIFE GOALS AND HOW DO THEY HELP?

Perhaps the first thing we should discuss is what life goals are. Take a minute to do the following exercise. It will clarify what I mean.

A Look Back from the Future

Picture yourself lying on your deathbed and a trusted friend or family member asks, "Did you accomplish what you wanted to in life?" Your answer helps point to what your life goals are. Life goals are the primary things that you want to accomplish over the course of your life, resulting in life fulfillment.

You might reasonably ask what I mean by "life fulfillment." What would make you satisfied that you had achieved what you wanted in your life? Those whom I have interviewed often describe life fulfillment as a sense of meaningfulness or purpose to one's life. Tina Sung, vice president of government transformation and agency partnerships for the Partnership for Public Service, described this as "making a difference—a difference to employees, to family, to customers and partners, to government and hopefully, to the world in some way."

Growing up in New York City as a child of Chinese immigrants, she had this idea that she wanted to break new ground. Her hard work in school got her into the first female class at Princeton, and since that time, she has made a difference in many organizations, including many years of serving as a leader in government or not-for-profit organizations and as a mentor to executives in the private sector. She added, "You have to want to serve and commit part of your life to making a difference—in my case in government and the social sector. For me, it is fulfilling when someone comes up to me and says, 'You don't know me, but you really made a difference in my life.'"

What would indicate to you that your life had been meaningful? For Mahatma Gandhi, the great Indian leader, professional life began as an attorney after an English education that prepared him for this field. Along the way, however, he found a different calling. After experiencing apartheid in South Africa and witnessing so much inhumanity in his homeland of India, he found that fulfillment in fighting injustice. As a lawyer, he could craft inspiring arguments for why change needed to occur. But most deliberately, he allowed himself to be thrown off trains or refused lodging as a statement that rallied thousands of new followers. In India, he was willing to lead a hunger strike to rally support against the salt tax that was a severe handicap for millions of poor Indians. Fulfillment was not in acquiring money, power, or tangible goods; he got rid of those trappings. Instead, his fulfillment was seeing the oppressed freed from the bonds of colonialism—free to make their own choices and self-govern.[7]

Martin Luther King Jr. was a minister and civil rights activist whose life fulfillment came from being able to see an America where all races would be treated equally. While he was still young, he saw and experienced the many inequalities that existed between blacks and whites. King was inspired by Gandhi's philosophy of nonviolent protests. He tried to educate America about these inequalities through his powerful speeches. For King, life fulfillment came as he stood up to advocate for his values by leading the civil rights movement despite the many hardships he had to endure.[8]

You do not need to be Gandhi or King to make a difference or to have a fulfilling life. My junior high school science teacher changed my life. Before meeting her, I had not had a teacher who really inspired me. She opened my eyes to the possibilities of a career in science and did so in a fun, engaging way. She served as a role model—a vibrant person who could engage others and bring out the best in them. It changed my energy and focus, putting me on the path to a math-science specialty in high school that enabled me to find my sweet spot. Later, I realized that she did that for many others as well.

One exercise that has worked for some people is to picture a gravestone or plaque commemorating your life. What would it say? Would it say something you would be proud of? Would it inscribe something that was meaningful to you?

Imagine reading your obituary in the paper. Most obituaries are short and must describe the person's life and contributions in only a few paragraphs. What would you want yours to say? Take a break from this reading to write a hundred-word obituary. Take time to reflect on things that you believe would bring you happiness and contentment both now and later in life. The following is an example of one person's desired obituary.

Katie's Obituary

Katie L., 80, died in her sleep in Hoboken, New Jersey, on November 20, 2073. She was born in Mexico in 1993 and came to the United States in 2002 with her mother. She graduated from City University of New York in 2015 with a degree in education. Her career was dedicated to improving people's lives. She met the love of her life in 2018, married him, and had three children. Those who loved her remember her as a caring woman who always did what was best for others. She cared greatly about the well-being of her mother, her husband, and her children. She will be sadly missed.

Assuming you have written the obituary or have the key points in your mind, have the highlights you have written been achieved already, or are they aspirational? If you have achieved these things, congratulations! For most of the people interviewed, their obituary was aspirational, helping them clarify the direction they wanted to head in life. Even the self-indulgent Lancelot of Arthurian legend, when asked of his perfection by Guinevere, said, "Physically yes, Your Majesty. But the refining of the soul is an endless struggle."[9]

Now or Later?

Another question that I am often asked in my seminars is this: Does this mean we must defer all satisfaction, hoping it all comes together at our deathbed? Of course not! Life is to be lived and enjoyed as much as possible every day. The reason that I am stressing life goals so much at this stage is that many other approaches to career, family, or educational planning focus on more immediate goals, but they do not focus sufficiently on the longer-term big picture—the meaning of your life.

While I probably spent far too many hours in college debating the meaning of life, that time invested and subsequent reflections of meaning throughout my life have helped me recalibrate where I want to go. Although a few lucky souls have their lives fall into place, most of us have to think about and plan for where we want to be later in life, because every step along the way is either a building block or a misstep toward life satisfaction. Remember my earlier advice—there are no guarantees in life! You cannot perfectly plan every step or event that will make you ultimately fulfilled. But by carefully thinking about the process of becoming fulfilled, you can greatly increase the odds of not only getting to life fulfillment but experiencing a great deal of satisfaction along the way. This thought process and periodic reviews will enable you to navigate difficult times, life's blind alleys, and make changes earlier rather than later, thereby letting you have more fulfilling years along the way.

When making important decisions, think about your values and your life goals and see if any of the possible choices align with those. Figure 16 is a tool that many people find helpful for life goal planning. First and foremost, you cannot do this while standing in line at your bank or texting friends. This is an exercise that requires you to go someplace secluded and think deeply. It requires the right frame of mind. After all, this is your entire life you are thinking about.

Start with the exercises that I just described. If you were on your deathbed and looking back over your life, what would make you the most satisfied or fulfilled? If others were describing your life, what would you want them to say about you? This is not easy because many thoughts are likely to run through your mind. There is a temptation to write down many short-term goals. This might be helpful to get started, but at the end of the exercise, you want to arrive at two to four big goals. The other smaller goals or accomplishments can be later positioned within your overall plan, so do not discard them.

For example, two of my life goals are using my abilities to advance my profession and having someone who loves me deeply for as much of my life as possible. In my case, indicators of my professional goal might be that people in my profession would recognize me for my contributions to the field or that I would have produced tangible things (such as books and articles) that will live on in the field long after I am gone. One indicator of having achieved the latter goal is that I had spent lots of time with this person over as many years as possible. My loved one would be holding my hand while I was dying, or perhaps we would be passing together.

A major motivation for me in writing this book is to pass along a legacy of ideas and to help others enrich their lives. In my relationship goal, I am hoping to make a difference for my family; in my professional goal, I am hoping that people in my profession or in the world in general have better lives because of what I contribute. The important thing is coming up with goals that are meaningful to you.

CAN GOALS CHANGE?

One kind of question that I am frequently asked, especially by younger people, is this: What if my life goals change? What if I change my mind? Is this wrong? Of course not. We are living and learning beings, so as we learn more in life or our viewpoints change, we may desire to adjust or change our life goals.

When I was in my teens, I thought money would be one of my three or four life goals. But as I grew more mature, I realized that money was more of an artifact and at most an enabler of some other activities I enjoyed. There is nothing wrong with money per se because many people with money make great contributions to society, but for me I realized that if not managed well, money could become a distractor to my true life goals. So money was taken off my life goal list and placed as an enabler of my life goals, which I will discuss later.

Life goals do change for many people and that is why I will introduce a process for how to keep them fresh throughout your life. This is not a one-time event, so please do not become too stressed over "getting it right." These are your goals, and they can be adjusted at any time. After all, you are the captain of your own ship. What is important is going through the thinking process periodically so that life does not pass you by without you having given your goals a thought. Also, this exercise should be a personal one. Copying someone else's goals or doing this as a group project doesn't really work. However, it can be extremely helpful after you take your first pass to sit down with someone whom you trust deeply and talk about what you have come up with. Better yet, if you can agree to complete this process with someone you trust deeply, it is then helpful for each of you to share what you have and discuss why and how it will help you achieve your fulfillment.

Figure 16 provides the life goal planning exercise, and figures 17 and 18 show examples of completed charts. In the spaces provided, list the two to four life goals that you would like to reach. In the column to the right, list indicators of what that would look like. After you have completed your life goal exercise, we will dig deeper into how to achieve them.

Balancing or Integrating Your Life Goals

Before we leave the setting of life goals, take a moment to reflect on their balance. Balance means having life goals in different aspects of your life—perhaps professional or work related; social, personal, or family related; physical or health related; financial related; and so forth. We often find that one-dimensional people are at first seen as successful, but upon further reflection, we realize that they often have something missing in their lives.

Figure 16. Life Goal Planning Exercise

Your Life Goals	Life Goal Indicators
1.	
2.	
3.	
4.	

Note: If you want to complete this online, go to http://www.wschiemann.com/fulfilled for sample worksheets and additional information.

FIGURE 17. Example of Life Goals and Indicators for Ira

Your Life Goals	Life Goal Indicators
1. Finding a life mate	Having many years of being with someone who is my soulmate
2. Being financially secure	Having enough money that I never have to worry about my financial well-being
3. Becoming famous	I would like to be recognized anywhere I go
4. Being recognized for my contribution to my profession	I would like people to reference me and my work for the value it added to society

FIGURE 18. Example of Life Goals and Indicators for Bridget

Your Life Goals	Life Goal Indicators
1. Being with and marrying a significant other who loves me	Being with that person many years Feeling comfortable and happy around that person despite being with them for many years
2. Being able to financially support my family	Having a job that allows me to provide a comfortable lifestyle for my mom and children
3. Being successful and taking on a career that I enjoy	Being in a job that makes a difference in the lives of others Being in a job that I find interesting and feel capable of doing
4. Travel	Visiting other countries and learning about other cultures

However, balance does not mean that we must always have different life sectors fighting against each other. Steward Friedman suggested that it is better to have integration across the various sectors.[10] Andre Agassi, the famous tennis star, reflected how inwardly unhappy he was despite being a tennis prodigy. He had felt pushed by family and coaches to excel, moving away from home at age thirteen.

In an interview, he said he hated tennis because of what it did to his family life and childhood. He dropped out of tennis in his twenties after sinking in rankings from number one to number one hundred forty-one in 1997, plagued by injuries. After much soul searching, he ultimately decided that he did want to go back to tennis—but on his own terms. The goals had to be ones he owned, practice was the path to getting there, and the motivation came from within—not outside. He went on to compete in many more Grand Slam tournaments, winning five, as well as scores of other tournaments. He regained his number one ranking in 1999 and is widely viewed today as someone who brought incredible passion to the sport. But he also speaks highly of finding the love of his life, Steffi Graf, likewise the preeminent female player of that period (at this writing, she still holds the record for the most weeks ranked as the number one female player in the world), with whom he could share—not dominate—experiences. He went about integrating his values, goals, and behaviors to create fulfillment. He sees his life after tennis as an opportunity to impact people for a lifetime (his schools, his foundation), whereas in tennis he would do so for just a couple of hours at a time.[11]

Many corporate examples of this abound as well. For too many executives of the Greatest Generation and the baby boomer generation, their life model was what William Whyte labeled the "organization man"—a person dedicated to success defined by his or her role in the organization.[12] Many CEOs and executives describe broken marriages, lost relationships with their children, and forgotten sports or hobbies all in the interest of climbing the corporate ladder. When many of them retired, they found emptiness. They were no longer the honchos of their prior world, which extended to golf clubs, social events, and other areas of constant recognition that they had achieved at the pinnacle of corporate life. Instead, many found that they needed to find soul mates, repair broken family relationships, and find meaningful ways to spend their time. The title and money alone were not creating fulfillment.

Today, many millennials are actively replacing this old model with one that is multidimensional, integrating family events, social media friends, organizational commitments, staying connected, health and exercise, hobbies, and volunteer activities. Many are finding fulfillment in variety and balance achieved through effective integration of varied parts of their lives.

What is the balance in your life? How well are you integrating important parts of your life? Take a look back at your life goals and ask yourself whether your goals are balanced and integrated.

A BALANCED FRAMEWORK

Dave Ulrich, the human resources guru and coauthor of *The Why of Work* with his psychologist wife, Wendy, said, "Be balanced in your choices: physical, social, emotional, intellectual, spiritual."

The life goals of many people appear to fall into six primary segments:

1. Career/occupational/job
2. Relationships, social and family
3. Education, learning, and personal growth
4. Leisure such as hobbies and sports
5. Spiritual, religious, and community
6. Hygiene, such as eating, sleeping, and health

While not a life goal per se, we are all constrained by biological necessities such as sleeping, eating, and exercising. I have certainly met individuals for whom one of these activities is a life goal or a critical part of their life fulfillment. I have known gourmands who live to eat and a former IT technician who was obsessed with time in the gym to be all he could be physically.

Figure 19 provides a way for you to think about some important goals you might have in each of these areas.

You will note that for most people, the pie chart in figure 19 is really more like the Venn diagram in figure 20, in which different parts of your life overlap. These segments of the pie are often competing for your time and energy: occupational versus family

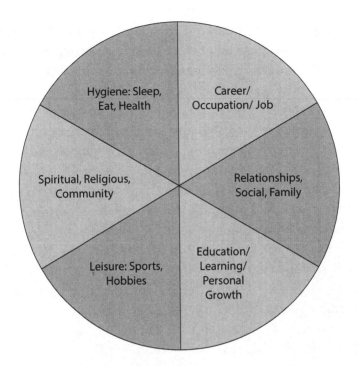

FIGURE 19. What Is the Right Balance for You?

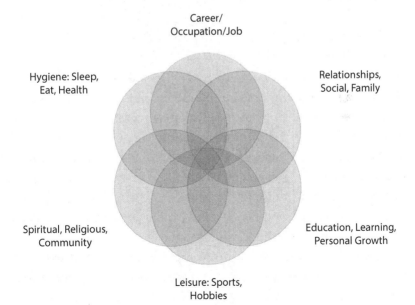

FIGURE 20. Venn Diagram: How Do You Mix the Key Parts of Your Life?

time, or perhaps social time versus hobbies. Do you find a good balance between spending time with friends and spending time with relatives? Do you have good balance between work and hobbies or relaxation?

Some people find ways to combine these goals or to mix their elements. More and more, we are moving into an integrated world in which different segments of our lives are blended together. For example, the line between work and home life has blurred for many employees, while some individuals now find ways to pray, practice yoga, or engage in spiritual activities at work. Many high-tech companies have fostered innovation by combining play and work. Google has a bowling alley for teams to mix play and team development. Many organizations that want to foster innovative ideas, such as advertising agencies, research groups, or software design teams, have games such as foosball or ping pong tables, allowing their employees to mix play and work, often producing great ideas.

Ask yourself if you have long-term life goals in some or all of these areas. What percentage of your time would you ideally like to spend in each of the six major segments?

What-How Thinking

Now that you have thought about your life values and life goals, it is possible to look at them side-by-side or put them into a matrix such as the one in figure 21. The columns represent life goals (*the what* I am seeking) and the rows represent life values (*the how* I will live my life while achieving those goals). We each must ask ourselves if we are being true to our values in every aspect of our lives.

For example, in figure 21, each of those goals—finding a life mate, becoming rich and famous, and making a contribution—must be consistent with your values: being ethical, honest, fair, and caring for others. There are a variety of ways to become rich, but not all of them involve doing it in a way that is consistent with the four values listed.

FIGURE 21. Goals-Values Alignment Example

		The What (Life Goals)			
		Finding a Life Mate	Being Rich	Becoming Famous	Being Recognized for My Contribution in My Profession
The How (Life Values)	Being Ethical				
	Being Honest				
	Being Fair				
	Caring for Others				

A blank goals-values template is included (fig. 22) for your use with your own goals and values.

A good test before moving on is whether you think you can achieve your life goals in a manner that is consistent with your life values. Look at the intersection of each goal and value and identify goals that may be difficult to accomplish while living your values. It is important to have a conversation with yourself about how you will resolve this conflict. If you don't, it will come back to haunt you later. One person I know backed away from a career in law enforcement because he was uncomfortable with conflict;

FIGURE 22. Life Goals Alignment Template

The What (Life Goals)			
The How (Life Values)			

he preferred switching to a career that was more collaborative, an important value to him.

LIFE GOAL GAPS

A key question that is begging to be answered is this: How do you get from where you are today to your life goals? First, you need to figure out where you are today and then do a life gap analysis to understand to what degree you have to move or adjust your current life path in the time you have available to steer in the right direction.

Let's go back to our Olympic example, since the 2012 Olympics were in session when I began writing this. These particular games attracted the largest audience in the United States of any Olympic contest in history—340 million viewers reported by NBC. It also featured the largest representation by countries (204) and the most female athletes ever.

In order for swimmer Missy Franklin to break international or Olympic records, she had to focus on where she was at a particular point in time and compare that to an existing record or benchmark. How could she shave time off already impressive records? For the most part, athletes today have equal access to dynamically engineered swimsuits or running suits, the best running or jumping shoes, or similar poles for vaulting. The Olympics is about people using the same tools and time (they each have twenty-four hours a day) to achieve their goal by managing the drivers of those goals—things such as working hard, building the right muscles, undergoing disciplined training, or getting advice from the right advisors and coaches. If your gap is shaving off 1.57 seconds in the butterfly stroke, you should focus on all the ways you can save time—stronger muscles, cleaner strokes, fewer strokes, and so forth.

So that is where we all must begin, knowing where we are today and measuring that against our goals. And remember, this thinking works at every age, from teenagers to centenarians. It is natural for teenagers reading this to have many uncertainties. Many high school students are beginning to think (or are encouraged by their parents to think) about potential careers, but career planning should be strongly connected to thinking about life goals and lifestyle.

A young woman I once knew loved to travel, go to concerts, and participate in several expensive hobbies. The problem was that she didn't integrate these interests into a life plan. She didn't effectively identify careers that would fit this lifestyle, and none of her pastimes seemed to be connected to a greater life purpose. What would make her fulfilled? Consequently, she continued to seek short-term relationships, opted for disjointed college courses that didn't lead to a career goal, and took jobs that produced money in the short term but had little long-run promise. She is not alone.

In contrast, my mother-in-law is an example of someone who was still excited to fulfill life goals—her bucket list—when she was in her seventies, eighties, and nineties. After my father-in-law died, she continued to work at the National Institutes for Health (NIH) with her friends. She took trips that required flying—something her husband couldn't do—to places like Hawaii or the jeweled Seychelles Islands, which were two of her dream destinations. When she retired after fifty years of service—a record at the time at NIH—she didn't retire from life. She started volunteering in her eighties at a senior center and helped keep their store running. She kept her home because it contained her garden, another avocation, and she kept traveling into her nineties to see sites in Europe and around the United States—places she had read about or heard about for many years. Whenever I asked her about going to a new place, her response was, "I'm ready!"

Where Are You on the Road to Your Life Goals?

So let's assess where you are on your life goal path. Figure 23 provides a template for self-assessment against your life goals. For each life goal, rate how close you are to achieving your life goal on a scale of one to ten, one being lowest—you are not at all close—and ten meaning you have already achieved it.

It is okay that your ratings are a rough estimate because only you can rate your progress against your vision of what a ten would be. In some cases, you might want to get feedback from others, such as a coach or mentor. The gap (ten minus the number you give it) represents the distance that needs to be closed to hit your life goal.

Figure 24 provides a sample of a completed template for Bridget, whom I introduced earlier in this book. Her two most important life goals are being with someone she loves and being successful in a career she enjoys. She still needs to define that, as well as take actions that will lead her to finding a significant other. The next chapters will talk more about how she will achieve her goals and how you can achieve yours.

FIGURE 23. Life Goal Assessment

Life Goals	Today's Rating
1.	
2.	
3.	
4.	
5.	
6.	

FIGURE 24. Sample Life Goal Assessment for Bridget

Life Goals	Today's Rating
1. Being with and marrying a significant other who loves me	6
2. Being able to financially support my family	3
3. Being successful in a career that I enjoy	6
4. Seeing the world	3

7

Stepping-Stones

What Are Your Lighthouse Goals?

*It's a lot easier to cross the river if you know
where the stepping-stones are.*

—Anonymous

LIGHTHOUSE GOALS

Unlike the fictional Superman, most of us can't leap in a single bound to our goals. We find it helpful to identify intermediate lighthouse goals. I use the term *lighthouse* because ships do not usually seek to hit the lighthouse—it is not their ultimate goal. Instead, the lighthouse provides assurance that the ship is on course and helps the captain avoid shoals and enter the harbor safely. The ancient Phoenicians and Greeks used lighthouses while sailing around the Mediterranean to ensure they were on course.

Most athletes also set intermediate goals for themselves, perhaps reducing their times in increments of minutes for a marathoner or in fractions of meters for a pole-vaulter. Another way to think about lighthouse goals for these athletes—or for any of us, for that matter—is by comparing them with some standard along the way. When my niece Lindsay was ice skating competitively, she realized that she was competing not only in absolutes (landing a triple Lutz) but also in comparative performance against others. The gold medal in the Olympics goes to the fastest sprinter, the best shooter, the highest jumper, and so forth, whether they break a world record or not. If your goal is setting a world record, you may be happy with getting a gold medal at the Olympics but experience some disappointment for failing to break the world record.

My father-in-law was a jewelry maker who had exacting standards for his work. Customers might praise a particular piece of jewelry, but if he knew that piece had a flaw, he felt compelled to tell them. If it was his own work, he would destroy it rather than sell something that didn't meet his standards. He said he could sleep at night if he knew everything he made met his high standards. He, not his customers, was the ultimate judge of whether he met the goal. He was living his values. His life goal of excellence would not have been achieved without hitting the intermediate, or lighthouse, goals of producing excellent jewelry.

Figure 25 shows an example of lighthouse goals for different life goals, including two that Bridget, whom we are tracking in her fulfillment quest, told us in the last chapter were important: success in a respected profession she enjoys and being surrounded by a loving family. Her master's degree will be one credential that will allow her to work for a large organization, perhaps in human resources, or in a consulting firm similar to the one she worked for prior to going back to school. If she had desired to be a licensed psychologist doing clinical work, she would then have to go back into a doctoral program. These are important decisions shaped by the end goal.

As I will repeat throughout this book, this is not a permanent career choice. One of my colleagues went back to get a PhD after running an auto parts business for years. I know other people with a degree who started working for a large organization and later chose to bring those skills and experiences to a start-up.

For example, take Condoleezza Rice, the former secretary of state serving under President George W. Bush. She was born in Birmingham, Alabama, and raised as a person of color in the segregated South. She lived in a community where black people were discriminated

FIGURE 25. Life Goal with Supporting Lighthouse Goals

against—shunted to special sections of buses or areas of a restaurant, assuming they could even go into that restaurant. She witnessed black children attending poor black schools with limited resources and teachers, while white children went to the best schools and had superior resources. People of color were lucky to not be beaten up, tortured, or psychologically scarred when crosses were burned on their lawns.

And yet, she escaped this environment with a clear vision that she shared with her father, who was a teacher and minister. She told him she wanted to become president of the United States. He didn't laugh or discourage her; he told her to go for it and that she could achieve whatever she wanted if she worked hard enough and had a clear focus. Although she didn't achieve the presidency as of this writing, she came quite close, holding one of the highest offices in the

land—fourth person in line to assume the presidency if the vice president, speaker of the House of Representatives, and the president pro
tempore of the Senate become incapacitated. She realized that she had
to achieve some intermediate goals to get to her ultimate goal: scoring
high grades in school, creating a résumé of service in public life, studying at the University of Denver and Notre Dame, taking courses in
Russian at Moscow State University, and subsequently holding a fel-
lowship at Stanford University. This relationship with Stanford would
continue as she was later appointed as an assistant professor there in
political science—an excellent launching pad for achieving a career
as a top-level statesperson. Her intermediate goals lined her up for a
high office. Was it a guarantee? No, but it placed her among the elite
prospects for such a role.

It is also worthy to note that Condoleezza is not a one-
dimensional person; she didn't start out knowing exactly what she
wanted her career legacy to be. In fact, she began taking piano lessons with the goal of becoming a concert pianist. She enrolled early
at the Aspen Music Festival and School and began her college career
as a music major, but she switched gears when it became clear that
she probably would not be able to compete professionally. However, to revisit my earlier remarks about balance, she continued this
avocation and often played with a chamber music group. And lest
you think this was playing for her dad in the drawing room, she
accompanied cellist Yo-Yo Ma in playing Brahms's *Violin Sonata
in D Minor* at Constitution Hall for the National Medal of Arts
Awards in 2002.[1]

As I am discussing lighthouse goals, I hope you are thinking
about what will cause your life goals to become reality. Lighthouse
goals provide a beacon to your life fulfillment, like the lighthouse to
a ship searching for its safe harbor. The lighthouse does not ensure
the ship will avoid all of the rocks or get into the harbor safely, but
it helps the captain determine if the ship is on course. But what
powers us to these lighthouse goals?

A number of success drivers contribute to reaching both lighthouse and life goals (see fig. 26). Again, they will not guarantee or

FIGURE 26. Success Drivers Support Lighthouse Goals and Life Goals

lock in that achievement—the real world throws many curve balls—but they increase the probability that your life goals will be reached.

SUCCESS DRIVERS

What do I mean by success drivers? What do they look like? In this section, we will take a look at some examples that I hope will encourage you to identify several drivers related to the life goals you developed in the previous chapter. Figure 27 provides some examples of success drivers that are related to the lighthouse and life goals in figure 25.

Success drivers (see the left side of fig. 27) are designed to steer us toward our lighthouse and life goals. For example, Condoleezza Rice was building her case for a role beyond being a judge through her undergraduate and graduate education by studying Russian and taking time to specialize in Soviet studies and Russian politics. This enabled her to network with people like George Shultz, Ronald Reagan's secretary of state, and Brent Scowcroft, who advised Gerald Ford and George H. W. Bush on national security, ultimately bringing her to the attention of the White House.

For an example of how this might translate for Bridget, who we have been following in her life fulfillment quest, see figure 28.

"Being successful in a respected profession that I enjoy" (fig. 28) is one of Bridget's life goals. She needs to consider what the pathways to success are. For example, she might choose to become a successful human resources professional. This field is becoming more important because it helps organizations manage talent—one of the biggest competitive differentiators for organizations today. The Bureau of Labor Statistics projects a 20.5 percent growth in employment between 2010 and 2020 for human resource positions. *USA Today*

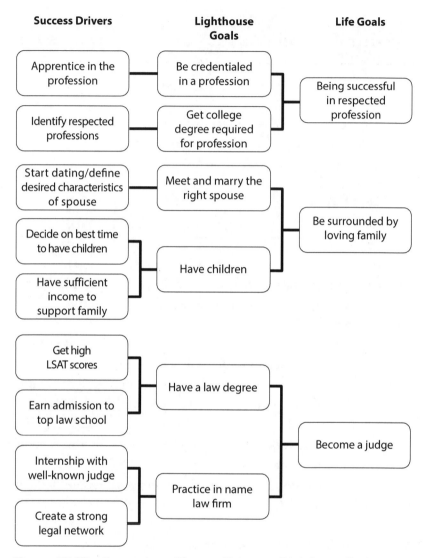

FIGURE 27. The Connection of Success Drivers to Lighthouse Goals to Life Goals

said that the role of human resources specialist is the sixth fastest growing job in the United States.[2, 3]

For that career, what will be required to be successful? College degrees in psychology are frequently good entry points. More and more, an advanced degree is becoming a differentiator for HR as

FIGURE 28. Bridget's Life and Lighthouse Goals and Success Drivers

Success Drivers	Lighthouse Goals	Life Goals
Define desired characteristics of spouse	Being with someone for many years who I am happy with	Being surrounded by a loving family
Start dating	Marrying someone who I know loves me	
Explore possibilities as a volunteer and intern	Having a job in which I will make a sufficient income	Being able to financially support my family
Seek out advisors and mentors		
Decide on desired profession	Getting a degree related to my career goal	Being successful in a respected profession that I enjoy
Pursue higher education		
Get broad-based experience as employee		
Study foreign languages and cultures	Having a job that allows me the time and financial ability to travel to other countries	Seeing the world
Join travel and sightseeing clubs		

well as for other professions. While there were few advanced HR degree programs a few years ago, schools such as University of Minnesota, DePaul, New York University, Florida International, Hawaii Pacific, and Marymount now offer master's degrees in this growing field.

Next, experience is important. Most often, you will start in a specialty part of HR, such as benefits management or recruiting. However, staying in one narrow area within HR is not a good predictor of future success for more senior positions. Most of the top HR leaders have had varied experiences across HR specialties or outside of HR. So planning for rotations into related opportunities to excel may be an important success driver.

Finally, the fields such as HR, law, accounting, project management, psychology, and engineering are increasingly demanding credentials (e.g., licensing or certification) and rewarding those who are credentialed with higher starting salaries. A good reason to focus on experience first is that some of the credentialing organizations require demonstrated experience before testing. So if Bridget chooses to leverage her psychology degree in the field of human resources, she will need to think about interning with firms to get some experience to add to her degree. That experience in turn will allow her to become credentialed as well as open doors to different types of work (benefits, organizational development, training) and organizations (government, business, consulting).

THE FIVE WHATS

These are examples of the kind of cause-and-effect reasoning that will help you think about how to get to your lighthouse and life goals. Some goals are more intangible, such as being respected in your profession. For those, you will need to think about the chain that helps you get to the life goal from prior actions (taking a course) and lighthouse goals (getting a degree). Start with your life goal and ask the five *whats*:

1. *What* are the intermediate steps that may be critical to achieving a life goal? That is, *what* lighthouse goals are important?
2. *What* are the success drivers you will need to achieve your lighthouse goals? This is where it often pays to get help from coaches or mentors, as well as to do research on the Internet.
3. *What* are some of the actions that would lead you to those success drivers? Are they actions you can take now?
4. *What* is your level of interest in those actions and success factors? If you don't have much interest in doing the things

that are on the critical path to your goals, then you will not be very motivated to complete the path.

5. *What* are the key competencies—aptitudes, abilities, knowledge, skills, experiences, and behaviors—required to do well in those actions and to achieve the success factors? If you do not have good aptitude for a particular path, then you soon will become frustrated and likely lose interest or motivation to continue along the path.

WHY ARE COMPETENCIES AND INTERESTS IMPORTANT?

In Part II, I discussed the ACE framework. Until now, I have mostly been talking about alignment of values, goals, and drivers of those goals. Competencies are part of the *C* component of ACE (capabilities) and an important ingredient for success. Level of interest is a strong contributor to the *E* component (engagement). It is hard to get excited about goals, values, and actions that do not match your interests.

Competencies refer to the aptitudes, knowledge, skills, abilities, experiences, and behaviors that you bring to work, relationships, and other activities in your life. They are the raw ingredients of success and fulfillment. These elements must come together in a fashion that creates value to you, an employer, a spouse, or others if you wish to be successful in any endeavor.

APTITUDES

Aptitudes are our underlying mental, physical, spatial, or perceptual strengths. They are predispositions based on our genetic makeup and early childhood experiences that make us stronger in certain areas, such as mechanical or spatial adeptness, even before we receive formal training. Without the right body type for swimming or running, the intellect for playing chess, or the tonal appreciation for performing music, achieving goals in those respective areas is unlikely.

Knowledge, Skills, and Abilities

Aptitudes alone are not enough. Most successes, career or otherwise, require a level of developed competencies—knowledge, skills, abilities, and experiences. For example, many manufacturing assembly jobs require manual dexterity. You need to be fast or flexible with your hands. Package delivery drivers require good spatial perceptions, especially if they are navigating complex city streets.

Knowledge is the acquired information that you have retained. Skills represent specific areas of competence that you have developed using your knowledge and abilities. For example, high SAT math scores are typically a good predictor of success in engineering careers, and they are often weighted more highly in engineering school admissions. Abilities measure developed aptitudes, just as the SAT exam measures verbal and mathematical abilities—a function of both aptitude and applied learning. However, one's ability to do math is only a prerequisite to successful engineering skills. Being able to design bridges, circuitry, or refinery processes requires acquiring specific skills that utilize your math abilities, along with the right knowledge. What are good design principles? What are design risks?

When I worked a summer job for Atlantic Richfield while in college, I took a course in automotive engineering and thought I really understood the inner workings of automobiles. Then, when I got under the hood of a car, I felt like I was in an Ellery Queen mystery. It all looked and felt different somehow. I didn't have the skills to tear down a carburetor yet. I knew what a Venturi tube was in a book, but seeing one and adjusting air fuel mixtures required combining my classroom knowledge and mechanical ability with what I learned from watching pros under the hood. By the end of the summer, I could adjust carburetors with the best of them—too bad most of that is done electronically today.

The problem with so many tests that students take is that those tests are not equally relevant to different individuals' goals. High

SAT scores alone will not make you a better auto repair person, a competent salesperson, or a talented painter. The willingness to put in the required rehearsal or practice time is essential. We know from work reported by Malcolm Gladwell in his best-selling book *Outliers* that there seems to be a "golden" ten thousand hours of practice that masters in many fields—musicians, chess masters, Olympic gold medalists—have invested.[4] Most virtuosos or experts in a variety of fields have devoted considerable time to developing their skills.

Remember, aptitude testing is more helpful in planning what you might be good at, but you have to recognize that both aptitude and developed competencies (knowledge, skills, abilities, and experience) are required to achieve success.

EXPERIENCES

When I worked on cars for my summer job in college, I developed my initial skills by observing master mechanics and then practiced, practiced, practiced. Through my mistakes and successes across many different types of automobiles, I became quite adept. If I had applied for a job requiring those skills, my experience applying those skills would have been viewed more favorably than someone who had received only classroom instruction.

BEHAVIORS

Within the area of competencies, everything I have talked about thus far is based on the past—your aptitudes, abilities, knowledge, skills, and experiences. This is the portfolio of success factors (or handicaps) that you bring with you each day. In contrast, behaviors are the here-and-now actions you perform daily—eating at certain times, reading the paper in the morning, exercising before or after work, performing the same activities day in and day out at your job—often not stopping to think about how these activities add value or how they support your life goals.

Human beings, like most species in the animal world, develop habits to cover routine things that we do all the time. Developing behaviors to deal with situations we encounter over and over is easier for our brains—no new processing. New behaviors are harder. They require thinking through the situation and drawing from your arsenal of knowledge, skills, abilities, and experiences to determine what behaviors are called for. However, this type of thinking and behaving has enabled us to adapt to changing circumstances. In fact, it is crucial to do exactly that in today's rapidly changing world.

Thomas Friedman, *New York Times* writer and author of *The World Is Flat: A Brief History of the Twenty-First Century*, makes two compelling arguments that affect each and every one of us with respect to adaptation. First, hundreds, perhaps thousands, of jobs are changing each year, with a sizable number of new requirements; in fact, most things around us are changing rapidly as we undergo one of the largest world transformations since the invention of the printing press more than five hundred years ago. Friedman attributes this to the convergence of globalization and technology, essentially changing many of the rules we have lived by over the past several hundred years.[5] Second, as I said earlier in this book, being average is over. While this may defy mathematical definitions of what *average* means, Friedman posits that an average worker could make a good living in an average job over his or her lifetime as recently as twenty-five to thirty years ago. Not anymore! He claims that being average will lead to substandard wages and lifestyles. The world is rewarding those who add a good deal of value through their uniqueness with high wages, reputation, and value and penalizing those who are marginally needed to produce goods, services, and so forth.

To Friedman's thinking, not improving one's knowledge, skills, and behaviors is tantamount to being marginalized in society. Life fulfillment for those who cannot change is likely to be limited at best.

INTERESTS

Most of us know someone whose parents pushed him or her into music lessons, a sport, or other activity in which they had low or no interest, only to discover later that the individual did everything he or she could to avoid practicing or spending time on the activity. Perhaps that was your experience. Regardless of your natural aptitudes, knowledge, skills, and experiences, if you are not interested in something, you are unlikely to be motivated to spend the time to excel at it. This is often the case of college students who switch majors after they have been encouraged by parents or teachers to become something that they had the skills for but lacked the interest in.

On the other hand, if you don't try new experiences, you may miss something you could love the rest of your life. I initially thought that I would dislike opera. But my wife "discovered" opera in graduate school almost by accident when a friend was working on sets for an opera company and asked her to come along. She heard *Tosca* and instantly knew that she had found something amazing. Her infectious enthusiasm (and prodding) finally got me to attend a performance at the Metropolitan Opera in New York City. After seeing Verdi's *Rigoletto*, I too was hooked. Don't miss out on opportunities to expose yourself to new possibilities that you may find transformative in art, music, auto repair, woodwork, gardening, pottery, yoga, or travel, which many of our interviewees told me came (to their delight) later in their lives.

My nephew has been hooked on producing music since he was an early teen. He was the lead guitarist and the youngest band member in a group that performed in New York City and surrounding areas. It was clear early on that he had not only an interest but a passion for music. While he had taken lessons for a horn, he took to guitar like a duck to water, practicing whenever he could. At one point, he was a member of two bands, having learned how to excel as a bassist as well. This enjoyable addiction went beyond performing. Michael and his dad built a fantastic studio in their basement, and he began to record, mix, and produce music for soloists and other bands. His early computer skills enabled him to quickly master the electronic musicology needed to produce studio recordings.

Unfortunately, unless you break through as an artist or join a major production studio, making a living in this field is a real challenge. My nephew smartly planned an alternative career that would be his backup—becoming licensed as an MRI technician. While he doesn't love the technician work as much as performing, the combination provides him both income and fulfillment.

A number of tests have been developed to help people determine their interests in different vocations based on their personal preferences or styles, such as the Kuder Career Interests Assessment, the Campbell Interest and Skill Survey, and the Strong Interest Inventory®. These tests help identify the interest side of the drivers of success. Intrinsic satisfaction is the satisfaction you feel simply by performing certain types of tasks or activities. What do you like to do without being asked or told to do it?

The Strong Inventory identifies six themes, and then a host of activities, that define the interests of different people. The six themes include these:

1. Realistic: Prefer working with tangible things and activities more than ideas or people.
2. Investigative: Like solving abstract or practical problems; less people focused.
3. Artistic: Like to work in settings where there are many opportunities for self-expression.
4. Social: Like opportunities to be sociable, responsible, humanistic, and concerned with the welfare of others.
5. Enterprising: Like selling, dominating, and leading; like social tasks where they can take control, have power or status.

6. Conventional: Prefer highly structured activities; dislike ambiguity, like to know exactly what is expected of them.

Research has identified which occupations are most connected to the interest themes and activities, thereby pointing to occupations that might be most suitable for different individuals. For example, the Campbell Interest and Skills Survey or the Strong Interest Inventory can show you how similar your interests are to the interests of people in each occupation. For more information on either of these two instruments, see https://www.cpp.com/products/strong/index.aspx and http://jca.sagepub.com/content/3/4/391.abstract.

Some people like doing more solitary or individually controlled work, while others like performing in teams. Some like high-communication activities, while others do not. When individuals perform tasks they enjoy, they experience satisfaction. I recently met a rug weaver in rural India who obviously took great pride in creating highly creative patterns. You could see him beaming as he described a family pattern and the detail work that goes into this craft. High interest does not guarantee full job satisfaction, however. I met another person in India who did handicraft work, but it was clear that this person did not have the same pride or fulfillment in doing the work. This person was working for a larger, impersonal firm. It was clear that he needed the money, but he did not have the same level of energy or enthusiasm.

Psychologists refer to extrinsic satisfaction as those things that bring satisfaction or dissatisfaction beyond the work itself. For example, the second person in this example may once have enjoyed the handicraft work (intrinsic satisfaction), but perhaps an overbearing boss, poor pay, long working hours, dirty conditions, or other factors reduced his extrinsic satisfaction. Overall job satisfaction requires both types of satisfaction—that which comes from the work itself and that which comes from surrounding factors—to be truly engaged in work or any other activity.

Today, children have an amazingly high degree of interest in playing video games. By age eight, 96 percent have watched TV, 90 percent have used a computer, 81 percent have played console video games, and 60 percent have played games or used apps on a portable device (cell phone, handheld gaming system, iPod, or tablet).[6] But how do we put all this interest in games to work?

Games alone may be enjoyable but may not lead to successful careers or add value to society, unless you are a developer of games. Luis von Ahn, a professor at Carnegie Mellon, is an innovative game creator who invented CAPTCHAs as a graduate student. (CAPTCHAs are the weirdly scripted combination of letters, numbers, and characters that you need to type into many websites to ensure that you are a human and not a computer trying to gain access.) From there, he went on to create interesting games that often served additional purposes. For example, he created a game for clarifying and verifying historical documents or digitizing old books or newspapers. Multiple combinations of two players compete to enter correct letters from these old scripts, thereby ensuring that often confusing, cloudy, or semilegible scripts are correctly identified by crowdsourcing the answers. While this may seem like work, when embedded into a game, work feels like play, and it draws hundreds of thousands of players—often for many hours at a time.

In one of his games, players are given pictures that they must describe by adding single words such as *house*, *sun*, *beach*, or *dog*. At the time he created this, computers were not very good at describing images. Each player competes with other players around the world who are looking at the same pictures. When they add words that are unique about the picture—the less common words—they get more points. In doing so, they are digitally describing pictures so they can be catalogued in a way that will be meaningful for searches in the future. Von Ahn has told us[7] that he had to set a maximum time that players could compete before the program cut them off. At the time, it was usually about sixteen hours, revealing that people were highly motivated to perform a verbal and spatial matching activity while developing their own levels of competency.

Here's the point: games draw people in because they are intrinsically interesting and offer some form of extrinsic reward, such as points or credits. What draws you in this way? What type of work might truly appeal to your interests? Jobs are changing in many ways, and people are making their own opportunities. Here are a few examples, led by hard work and passion:

- In my area, many Vietnamese immigrants who came to this country with almost nothing now own and operate their own businesses, such as Dunkin' Donuts.
- My local café was started by a Chinese man who had little experience in the coffee or tea business, but his passion was coffee, tea, and people. He wanted to create the best tea and coffee experience, outpacing Starbucks. His small café was a quick success.
- An intern of mine has an uncle with one year of high school education who created a trucking company. He loved driving, and by working different factory jobs, he was able to purchase a truck and make furniture deliveries. He now has seven large trucks and does deliveries for well-known companies.
- One woman I know enjoys arts and crafts. She began to volunteer at nursing homes doing arts and crafts programs. Now this has become her primary job. She is paid to come to various nursing homes.
- A childless couple I know always wanted to have children and loved taking care of children for neighbors and friends. One day they said, "Why don't we do this as a business?" The wife quit her job and worked a daycare start-up, using money her husband was still bringing in. After they got one daycare center off the ground, they

had such high demand for their services that the husband soon quit his job to join in the expansion. They are now part of a burgeoning industry.[8]

In the case of Bridget, she has an interesting mix of competencies and interests. She is quite strong analytically but also enjoys being around and working with people. This might not bode well for being in a more isolated job, such as a benefits or compensation analyst in HR. But it might suggest she would do well in training or personal organizational development, where she would be called on to work with managers and employees to improve teams and organizational effectiveness.

IDENTIFYING YOUR CRITICAL INGREDIENTS TO FULFILLMENT

Take time now to identify what success drivers might be important for each of your life goals. Don't rush this because each driver will lead to your taking actions that support it, and it will be frustrating to start down a path of actions that ultimately arrives at a dead end. After you select your drivers, identify the important actions you might need to take to reach the drivers. A completed example for someone with a life goal of becoming a judge is shown in figure 29. (A complete life goal map covers multiple aspects of one's life; this will be discussed in more detail in Chapter 8.) A blank template is provided in figure 30 for you to enter your interests, competencies, actions, success drivers, lighthouse goals, and life goals.

SUMMARY

Multiple factors go into reaching one's goal, but pursuing some to the exclusion of others may reduce the chances for success. This is why I encourage young adults or those early in their career to develop multiple interests, hobbies, and avocations; one's aptitude

FIGURE 29. Example of Life Plan for Becoming a Judge

Interests	Competencies	Actions	Success Drivers	Lighthouse Goals	Life Goal
Learning about nutrition and exercise	Has knowledge of healthy habits	Stay healthy	Get high LSAT scores	Have a law degree	Become a judge
Social activities	Has had trouble being able to limit time with friends and spend more on school work	Limit social time			
Not very interested in classes required to get into law school	Has struggled with SAT scores previously; undergraduate grades C+/B-	Get high grades	Earn admission to top law school		
Very interested in the social interactions	Is approachable and able to discuss different topics	Take courses that increase verbal skills	Internship with well-known judge	Practice in name law firm	
Not very interested in talking about legal issues	Must be able to talk about yourself and your legal knowledge	Network with regional legal professionals	Create strong legal network		

FIGURE 30. Factors That Will Influence Your Lighthouse and Life Goals

Interests	Competencies	Actions	Success Drivers	Lighthouse Goals	Life Goals

may prove to be a good match for certain interests, career aspirations, or life goals, but not for others.

Regardless of your stage of life, having a clear path from today's actions to your drivers, lighthouse goals, and life goals is essential. However, this life path has to be realistic given your aptitudes, interests, knowledge, skills, and prior experiences.

8

A Picture Is Worth
a Thousand Words

*Every now and then one paints a picture that seems to have
opened a door and serves as a stepping stone to other things.*

—Pablo Picasso

As Dorothy said in the Wizard of Oz, "I want to go home," but
she didn't know how to get there.[1] In the previous chapter, I talked
about identifying the key success drivers and lighthouse goals that
will help you achieve your life goals. In this chapter, I want to review
those drivers for balance and relevance. You don't want too many
(more than you can manage) or too few (not enough to help you
reach your goal).

Also, the adage that a picture is worth a thousand words aptly
applies here. You may find it helpful to develop a picture that
can illustrate how your drivers will get you to your goal. In this
chapter, I will share how these pictures, or life maps, will enable
you to see your overall life road map. At the same time, you will
be able to zone in on where you are today and the things you
need to do now. Once again, this picture, like many in life, needs
constant adjustment as life tosses new challenges or opportunities your way. It will be important to update the picture as time
moves on.

REVIEWING DRIVERS FOR BALANCE

Before we leave drivers and move to our finished life map, we want to make sure that we have considered how balanced our drivers are. I discussed the concept of balance in the first chapter in this section. Just as we talked about the importance of balance in goals, so too must we think about balance in the drivers and the actions that support the drivers, as this will affect how we spend our time.

We can think of balance in several ways:

1. Balancing drivers of life goals
2. Balancing leading and lagging indicators
3. Balancing drivers over time

Let's take a look at each area.

BALANCING DRIVERS OF LIFE GOALS. Assuming you have created the right balance in your life goals, have you also balanced your success drivers and the actions that compete for your limited time? For example, let's consider someone who is aspiring to become a top-notch legal professional—perhaps a judge—as we talked about in the last chapter. Key drivers for this person might include high LSAT scores and admission to a top law school. Key actions to support the drivers might include getting high undergraduate grades and staying healthy.

Sounds pretty good, right? However, there is another dimension required of many in the legal profession or those who aspire to become a judge—relationships. Law, like many professions, is a contact sport. Successful lawyers are not typically wallflowers. They network, build relationships, and hone excellent communication skills. Good grades and a high LSAT score do not make up for a lack of communication skills or other relational skills and competencies. What might that mean for our aspirant? Perhaps success in debate classes might be important. Public speaking experience might be a good early indicator of future success. Having deep relationships, perhaps built through activities such as Rotary Club, religious groups, community volunteer activities, or other networking experiences, may be complementary to this profession.

While we don't want to jump to the specific actions in our plan yet, this should provide an example of how certain drivers—good communication and debate skills and strong relationships—could be important balancing elements to the formal school and intern track described initially. Another balancing factor may be family or social needs. Many great attorneys, engineers, and nurses talk about how critical a partner was during school and in the early stages of career development—having someone to talk to during difficult times or having someone who supports you when others do not. Perhaps having monetary support from a spouse, parents, or friends may enable you to attend college or afford a better school that aims your success trajectory closer to the target.

This notion of balance is not only for early career people; those switching careers, marriages, or social networks need to think about what they want for the rest of their lives. What kind of career would they want, knowing what they know now? What type of relationships are fulfilling? What hobbies capture your excitement and passion?

Remember, it is never too late to plan for the future. The now infamous high school chemistry teacher Walter White from the award-winning TV show *Breaking Bad*, a man dying of cancer with only months to live, planned for how he wanted to leave his affairs. He wanted to quickly earn sufficient money for his family and disabled son so they wouldn't have to live in poverty. He had the "what" he needed to do, but many would question "how" he chose to do it.

BALANCING LEADING AND LAGGING INDICATORS. The ultimate lagging indicator (an indicator is something that tells you the result or outcome) is your life fulfillment, which is closely related to achieving your life goals. This is preceded by a series of lighthouse goals and success drivers of those lighthouse goals, which in turn is preceded by how we spend our time every week.

What do I mean by "leading indicator"? Simply put, a leading indicator is something that helps us predict a future result. For example, in our legal example, it is impossible to get into law school without a bachelor's degree and high scores on the LSATs. Those are leading indicators of getting a law degree—a lighthouse goal. However, they are not a guarantee of it. A bachelor's degree is a necessary but not sufficient requirement to get into law school. You also need good test scores, strong references (remember your network), and the ability to articulate your reason and purpose for why a particular law school should accept you versus many others (remember communication skills).

It is important to think carefully about what the sequence of those leading indicators might be so that your near-term action plan addresses the near-term hurdles you must overcome. Some things cannot be developed at the last minute. You cannot grow deep professional relationships overnight, so work on this may need to begin early on. Relationship building is not like taking a course or even gaining a degree; it requires a long and steady course of action.

How can a young person with such aspirations know what the leading indicators are? Find and talk to attorneys. If you can find only one attorney initially, ask that attorney to connect you to others. Ask them what the road to success requires. Listen carefully for the ingredients needed along the way to become successful in that profession.

BALANCING DRIVERS AND ACTIONS OVER TIME. It is important to check whether you have a mix of short-, intermediate-, and long-term drivers. This balance is necessary so that there are immediate hurdles that you can focus on—ones that are in the line of sight between short-term actions and long-term goals. For example, if you want to be a master auto mechanic, it will be helpful to begin working on cars in your spare time, perhaps at home and then as a part-time job at a garage. Taking courses in high school or in adult education in mechanical skills might be a good early driver. A job with a dealership that will send you to school is another potential intermediate driver of getting to that master craft job.

In our earlier legal example, if a student is a junior in college, completing the degree with high grades and scoring high on the LSATs might be an important short-term driver of success. An intermediate driver might be building references and relationships. A long-term driver might be scoring a great internship.

If you are in midlife, the same kind of thinking can be applied. At this stage of your life, you may have some fairly good ideas of what you like and dislike. If you aspire to change jobs or careers, what aspects of your current situation are you trying to change—things that are not fulfilling? What jobs or roles have you observed over time that have intrigued you? Spend time searching the Internet to learn about some of those roles. Do some networking. While you could start from scratch at something new (and there's nothing wrong with that), it would be easier to make a shift into something that you already have a head start in.

One of my colleagues is an umpire in his spare time. He started out doing it for his kids and then got more and more involved. Now he umpires for various leagues. Could he make a shift into more professional umpiring? Who knows? But if he wanted to, he would already have some credentials and experience. Another colleague is a chef. He wasn't always a chef; he started out in a corporate job and realized it wasn't for him. He made tentative plans for a new lighthouse goal as a chef and then began taking actions on drivers of success in his spare time, such as assisting chefs at a catering business and taking cooking classes.

In the end, balance is an important factor to consider on these three different dimensions. Take another look at your drivers for each life goal and assess whether they are balanced on the previous criteria. Then make the necessary changes.

BUILDING A PERSONAL LIFE GOAL MAP

Take a look at the life goal map in figure 31 for becoming a judge. It shows the path to achieving this goal. Your own life goal map should capture your thinking today about your life path. If you have been following the process in the previous two chapters, you will not have far to go to connect the dots. On the far right will be your life goals. To the left of those will be lighthouse goals and success drivers. The way to construct the map is to start with the life goals on the right—your end objective—and work back to the left. What are the intermediate lighthouse goals that will steer you toward your life goals? In turn, what drivers are important to getting to the lighthouse goals?

For example, the goal of becoming a judge (fig. 31) on the right includes intermediate lighthouse goals (immediately to the left) of getting a law degree and practicing in a name law firm. To the left of practicing with a name law firm are drivers such as getting into a good law school, scoring high on LSATs, interning with a name judge, and having a strong legal network.

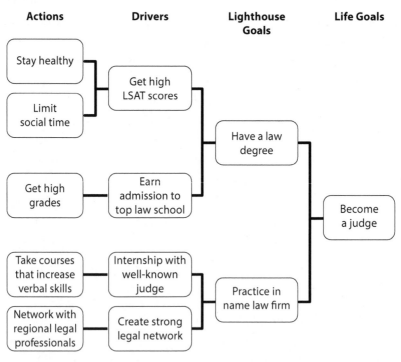

FIGURE 31. Example of Life Goal Map for Becoming a Judge

Building the plan starts on the right, but implementing your plan begins on the left because you have already built a logic chain of what is most important to do today (left) to get to where you want to go tomorrow (right). The drivers on the left are where you will want to focus your attention today. If the person who completed this map is three semesters from graduation with a bachelor of arts, then the immediate focus is on getting great grades in the remaining courses, learning things that will help them achieve high scores on LSATs, staying healthy, and curtailing social time to a level that will balance current enjoyment with continuing to make progress on the short-term critical path actions. Figure 32 provides an example for a different job—a preschool teacher. Once again, building the plan starts on the right, but implementing your plan begins on the left with actions you can start on today.

What you see more clearly when you do the mapping are the tradeoffs that we all make, explicitly or implicitly. How to balance social life with academic life? How to balance health with partying or unhealthy eating? How to balance family obligations with

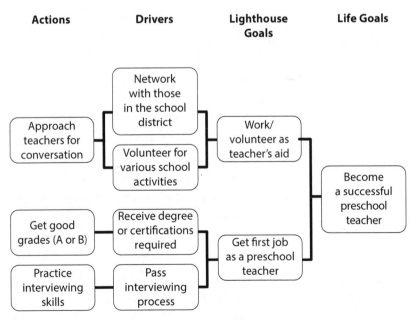

FIGURE 32. Example of Life Goal Map for Becoming a Preschool Teacher

career pursuits? We all make these tradeoffs because we all have only twenty-four hours in a day. The question is whether we do it consciously or not.

I know from personal experience. As I discussed in the introduction, I went to college and was like the kids in the movie *Willie Wonka and the Chocolate Factory*. I wanted to experience everything—listening to interesting professors, eating somewhere outside of home, talking with kids on my dorm floor, playing drums in my band, being a DJ at the campus radio station, playing pinochle to all hours of the night, and running for student government.

I wanted to do it all but didn't have a plan for how to balance all those desires. I was elected treasurer of the student government and life couldn't get much better—until I found myself on academic probation. I was in a state of shock. I realized that I did not have a plan that was connected to my goals; in fact, my life goals were fuzzy at best. Like many children and students, all through my life, I had had a clear path laid out for me—compete in band, get merit badges in Boy Scouts, finish elementary and high school, and get into college. Now what?

How did I get myself into this situation, and how could I get myself out of it? I realized then that I needed some sound thinking and good coaching. One friend whom I respected on my dorm floor was quite honest: "You don't study effectively and you goof off too much." Although he was not my type—way too studious at the expense of other interests—I realized that there was a lot of truth to his statement. The goof-offs on my floor told me to just forget the dean's list and it would all work out. I had reached a deciding moment in my life, and I didn't have life goals clearly in my head. My friend's coaching helped me realize that I really did want and need the degree from my university to do many things that I wanted to do later. I would need not just passing grades but strong grades.

After much soul searching, I calculated what I would need to do for my remaining five semesters—assuming they let me stay! This gave me some hope, because it was still technically possible to graduate with over a 3.5 grade point average—a split between an A and B—and a track record of great grades for my second half of college. Was I willing to do what it would take? Even with hard work, what were the odds of suddenly going from a B/C/D student to an A student?

But it was thinking about my map (although it wasn't as clearly articulated in my brain at the time) that changed my life. I knew I would be climbing a mountain and that there were no guarantees of getting into graduate school, of high graduate school entry exam scores, or even of getting a great job, but I had to try. I went back to that studious dorm mate and said, "Can I move in with you next semester?" I think I heard his jaw hit the table.

"*You* want to move in with *me*?" he said. "You? Do you realize how hard I study? Are you prepared to keep hours that don't disrupt my sleep or study habits?"

I said I recognized it but did not fully understand it and asked for his help to teach me how to become a better student. He reluctantly agreed; after all, I was a bad bet from my prior behaviors. But it was the turnaround of my life. I had a clear set of drivers that I needed to focus on:

- picking a major (I had already had three!) that I would enjoy
- taking classes that would stimulate me and would really prepare me for graduate school and the GREs
- taking on this colleague as a mentor and really giving a new study approach a fair chance
- taking on new friends who had similar drivers and lighthouse goals to mine and eschewing friends I was allowing to take me down a rat hole (most of them dropped out over the next year)
- learning new study habits
- keeping a smaller number of social and developmental hobbies that provided immediate fulfillment to balance my life (For example, I really wanted to be a good student council treasurer and even run for president in the future,

but gave up the radio station and limited my card playing to a specified number of hours per week.)

By the way, I later ran for president and lost by only a few votes, but I wasn't willing to put in the time that I had for treasurer at the expense of dropping out. Being president was far cooler than getting a straight-A semester, but I had reevaluated my priorities and needed to stick with my new plan. I was okay with the outcome because I was staying the course to my most important drivers of success.

CREATING YOUR MAP

If you have done a good job of identifying the drivers in the previous exercises, creating the map will be fairly easy and provide you with a snapshot of your life path today. As I have said throughout the book, this is not set in stone. Things change, but you should not expect your life goals to change radically in the short term. Your life may change after lifetime milestones such as getting married, having children, or losing a loved one, but the more you have thought about your life in the future, the less you will need to ditch your plan and make radical changes.

Take time now to put your life goals, lighthouse goals, and drivers into a map that shows the cause-effect relationship among them. Consider the following in putting it together:

- Do the life goals on the far right feel right when you look at the picture?
- Is it balanced? Consider short- and long-term drivers, leading and lagging indicators of success, and balance across your life at each stage. Have you balanced your social and career needs? Have you balanced short-term actions with long-term goals?
- Do you have a clear set of short-term drivers that you agree are the most important immediate areas to focus on?

One final question: Do you have the right number of life goals, lighthouse goals, and drivers? This is not a trick question and there is no magic answer, but from experience with mapping over the years at Metrus, I have learned a few things about successful maps. Too many elements and it becomes overwhelming and complex; too few and the odds are that you are leaving important parts of you out—perhaps you are thinking too narrowly.

If you have fewer than ten elements to describe your life path, it is certainly too few. If you have more than twenty-five, you are probably pushing beyond manageability. Having twelve to sixteen or so really important drivers and goals will be more effective than thirty minor drivers and goals that overwhelm you, causing you to lose focus. As you can see from the prior examples I have shared, one to three life goals are typical among those I have interviewed, with perhaps three to six lighthouse goals and five to eight drivers to steer you to the goals.

9

Where Are You Today?

The self is not something ready-made, but something
in continuous formation through choice of action.
—John Dewey, *The Middle Works, 1899–1924*

Armed with clear life and lighthouse goals, well-thought-out drivers of success, a life map, and good measures to assess progress, it is time to take stock of where you are on the journey toward fulfillment. The following are four cases that exemplify various life goals.

CASE 1: LIVE LONG AND HEALTHY

For the life goal of living a long and healthy life (fig. 33), which most of us can identify with, the map is constructed to help us visualize the path to the goal. To the far right is the life goal. Moving progressively to the left are lighthouse goals, then the drivers of life goals. For example, two lighthouse goals of the life goal here are "Avoiding diseases" and "Proactive health management." Drivers of these two lighthouse goals include the following:

- Frequent diagnostics of my health. Having the diagnostics (medical examinations) tell me if I am healthy or not, and if not, what is the gap or concern that needs to be

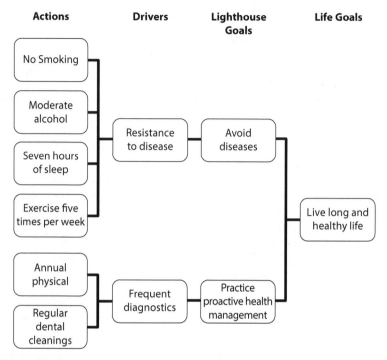

FIGURE 33. Example of Life Goal Map for Long and Healthy Life

addressed? For example, my parents, like many people who reach a certain age, take a drug to reduce their cholesterol. This need was identified by reviewing regular blood tests when they went in for their physical examinations. I may need to be vigilant about this risk.

- Resistance to disease. Various drivers of this might include giving up smoking, engaging in regular exercise, moderating alcohol consumption, practicing healthy eating habits, and getting adequate sleep. Each of these drivers has been the subject of many medical studies showing that there is a relationship between them and resistance to disease and longevity.

The drivers are a lot easier to measure, but we also have to recognize that not all disease resistance is within our control. Heredity plays a big role in some diseases such as Huntington's, Alzheimer's, and diabetes, among others.[1] Also, where one lives can be a factor. It has been reported that people living in close quarters as well as living in poor conditions are more susceptible to communicable diseases.[2] Where one travels can be another factor. For example, when my family traveled to several countries in Africa, we were required to obtain yellow fever vaccinations. The same was true of malaria, typhoid, hepatitis, and so forth.

The measures of most of the drivers are fairly straightforward:

- Drugs, alcohol, and smoking can be measured by amount and frequency.
- Obesity can be measured by weight relative to height (body mass index).
- Propensity to contract certain diseases can also be predicted by measures such as high blood pressure, which is connected to strokes, or high cholesterol, which can lead to heart disease.
- Healthy eating reflects the daily or weekly balance of essential food groups, including fresh fruits and vegetables and adequate sources of fiber.
- It should be recognized that there is no universal understanding of sleep requirements for different individuals. Some individuals seem to thrive on six hours of sleep a night and others require nine. One approach is to keep a sleep diary and see how varying lengths of time affect your daily functioning: alertness throughout the day, headaches, sex drive, moodiness, or performance at work.

CASE 2: RELATIONSHIP FULFILLMENT

For most of us, family or deep friendships are important. This was the number one or number two goal for a strong majority of people in my interviews. For some individuals I have spoken to, this is the paramount life goal.

Figure 34 displays a life goal map for relationship fulfillment. My aunt Marie, above all else, wanted to be loved not only by her immediate family but by her extended family, which included the scores of children and grandchildren of her sisters and brothers and of her mother's sisters and brothers—a large clan, to say the least. Another woman I interviewed saw children as a crucial life goal. She wanted as many children as she could have, and she pictured lying on her deathbed surrounded by this loving family who would honor her. She expected that these children would be a part of support group in old age when she would need help physically, mentally, and perhaps financially.

Bridget, whom you met earlier, identified a loving family as a strong life goal. To that end, the left side of the map is particular relevant for her. Being a bit introverted until she gets to know people, she realized that she would need to force herself to join social organizations to become a better networker and make time to date.

Similar to our other maps, on the far right is our life goal. To the immediate left are lighthouse goals such as having many children (her measure was the number of children and her target was three), having many grandchildren (she hoped for ten or more), as well

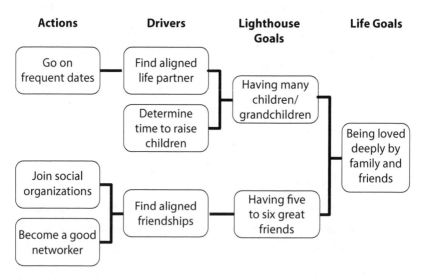

FIGURE 34. Example of Life Goal Map for Deep Love with Family and Friends

as good friends who would be with her into advancing years (she wanted at least five or six).

These lighthouse goals in turn required certain drivers such as finding someone to have children with and building a friendship network that produced a small number of good friends. This all required being socially active at an early age, in this case identifying a husband who wanted children and freeing up sufficient time in her life to get a family started and spend time with developing friends.

To accomplish this, she joined many social organizations, some related to dating. She liked being around many acquaintances (more than one hundred) hoping that good friends (and a husband) would emerge from this. She tried to go out on dates at least twice per week to ensure that she was meeting enough potential marital candidates who would share her goals.

Case 3: Career

In the previous chapter, we developed and displayed a life goal map for becoming a judge (fig. 29). The example is repeated here for completeness (figure 35); it was described in detail in Chapter 8.

Case 4: Avocation

Case 4 involves a man named Will who had two major avocational goals: travel and music. He had grown up reading travel books, devoured geography classes, and found cultural differences exhilarating. Like most people, he had to make some choices about what to focus on in his limited time. He settled on two big ideas: seeing the world and becoming a proficient musician. Other hobbies, such as reading, movies, and theater, would remain secondary.

He wanted to experience as much of the world as possible, and he knew he wanted to get started early. He also had a good musical history, participating in a school orchestra in elementary school and bands in high school and college. But he always wanted to spend

Figure 35. Example of Life Plan for Becoming a Judge

Interests	Competencies	Actions	Success Drivers	Lighthouse Goals	Life Goal
Learning about nutrition and exercise	Has knowledge of healthy habits	Stay healthy	Get high LSAT scores	Have a law degree	Become a judge
Social activities	Has had trouble being able to limit time with friends and spend more on school work	Limit social time			
Not very interested in classes required to get into law school	Has struggled with SAT scores previously; undergraduate grades C+/B-	Get high grades	Earn admission to top law school		
Very interested in the social interactions	Is approachable and able to discuss different topics	Take courses that increase verbal skills	Internship with well-known judge	Practice in name law firm	
Not very interested in talking about legal issues	Must be able to talk about yourself and your legal knowledge	Network with regional legal professionals	Create strong legal network		

more time with a musical instrument such as guitar or piano. Will didn't own a piano, but when he bought a house in which the prior owners left a piano, the opportunity was there. He took lessons as an adult, and no matter how tight his schedule was, he wanted to reach a certain level of proficiency, often practicing well after midnight. Figure 36 shows Will's life goal map.

Once again the life goals—in this case, two life goals—are displayed on the right in figure 36. Potential lighthouse goals included "rich cultural experiences" and "visiting at least one new country each year." These in turn had drivers such as becoming a great travel planner and having sufficient income or time to do this. And this required taking actions such as creating a bucket list of countries by priority and studying world sites to learn more about various regions.

Bridget, who also had a secondary life goal of seeing the world, needed to think about how that might play into her decision to

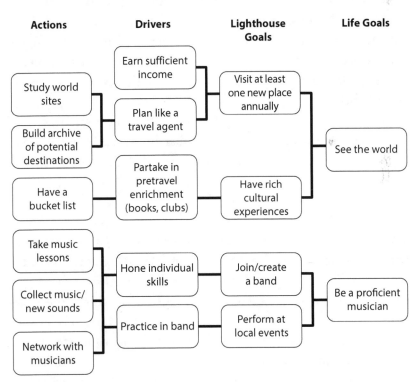

FIGURE 36. Will's Life Goal Map for Seeing the World and Musical Avocation

apply her psychology degree to human resources in a large corporation, a smaller consulting firm, or in a start-up business with her
brother. In the large corporation, she feared that limited vacation
time and flexibility would reduce her chances of doing much travel
for a while. And in the start-up, she realized she would be swamped
working eighty-plus-hour weeks, allowing almost no time for travel.
The small consulting firm looked more and more appealing from
that perspective because travel was a part of the job, and she would
have more flexibility in the structure of that firm.

With regard to his musical goals, after a passing fantasy of making a career in music, Will decided that playing music was more
fulfilling than writing or listening to it. Combined with his outgoing personality, performing music for live audiences was the most
exciting prospect. He had done quite a bit of this in orchestras and
bands early in his life. But he knew that he could not devote the
time to do that professionally. He was happy to perform at local
events (a lighthouse goal), which required him to form or join a
band (a lighthouse goal) and of course practice with them and hone
individual skills (drivers). He started down this path by taking music
lessons, listening to new sounds, and networking with other musicians (actions).

But Will had to manage the balance of his avocations as well as
his career, family, and health. This challenge eventually led to some
adjustments to his avocational goals, as we shall discuss shortly.

Are You Sure about Your Life Goals?

You may have wondered up to this point how one is so sure about
one's life or lighthouse goals. Might they not change over time? In
the case of Will, our traveler-musician, that is exactly what hap-
pened. Two things occurred to bring this about. First, the time
available to stay proficient at piano was dwindling due to his professional, family, and health goals. The activities that supported those
goals began squeezing out musical time. About the same time, Will
became interested in scuba diving. It was something he had read

about but never had a chance to experience. He loved the sea and began to see potential connections between his travel yen and scuba.

Once he was certified by PADI—a professional scuba diving certifying organization—he could dive anywhere in the world. And that is exactly what he did, combining his travel lust with a hobby that could complement it. In figure 37, we can see his adjusted goals, with scuba becoming the new avocation goal and lighthouse goals of making a sufficient number of dives to remain proficient and gaining advanced certification. These in turn were preceded by drivers such as getting basic certification, buying equipment, and planning trips with friends. But he had to begin with actions such as taking lessons,

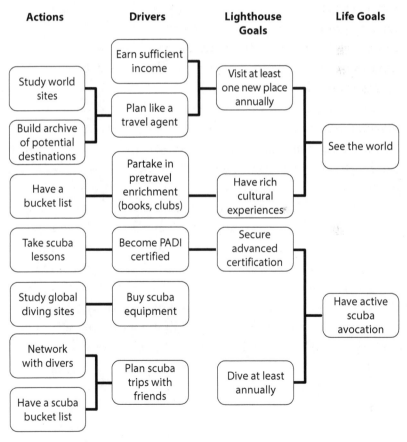

Figure 37. Will's Adjusted Life Goal Map

networking with divers, and studying global sites. This hobby also enabled him to connect to other minor avocations such as underwater photography.

Over time, scuba offered some other benefits as well. As his job intensified and he grew older, he needed vacations that provided more relaxation and rest. Scuba provided that outlet. While scuba diving is not for the faint of heart, it was possible for him to take more relaxing vacations than hiking through the Himalayas or spending twelve hours a day in the streets of Lisbon. He could spend half the day diving and the rest reading and relaxing.

Furthermore, diving brought him to new parts of the world. For example, when business brought him to Australia for work, he took stretch days to go up to Port Douglas to dive the Great Barrier Reef, thereby seeing one of the great wonders of the world—a fulfilling part of his travel dreams. Diving brought him to Polynesia, the Indian Ocean, the Caribbean, and the Pacific, thereby combining two avocations at the same time.

But planning can only get us so far. Reality often throws us a curve: a woman who cannot have children despite wanting them, a sports star who can't make the next performance level, someone with travel lust but without a budget. In the world of work, many of us face this throughout our careers—a job that doesn't work out, a promotion we didn't get, or a career that gets replaced by automation.

My uncle Don faced that exact situation when the printing industry moved from skilled craftspeople to automation. He had thought for sure he would retire in that well-paying industry. Instead, he had to make midlife career decisions, eventually landing in real estate, a field that played to both his smarts and his sociability.

My advice would be to recognize that good planning helps us chart a path to fulfillment, but we must always be prepared to adjust our plans to fit reality. Those with good plans, including backup plans, usually have more options when the tide turns.

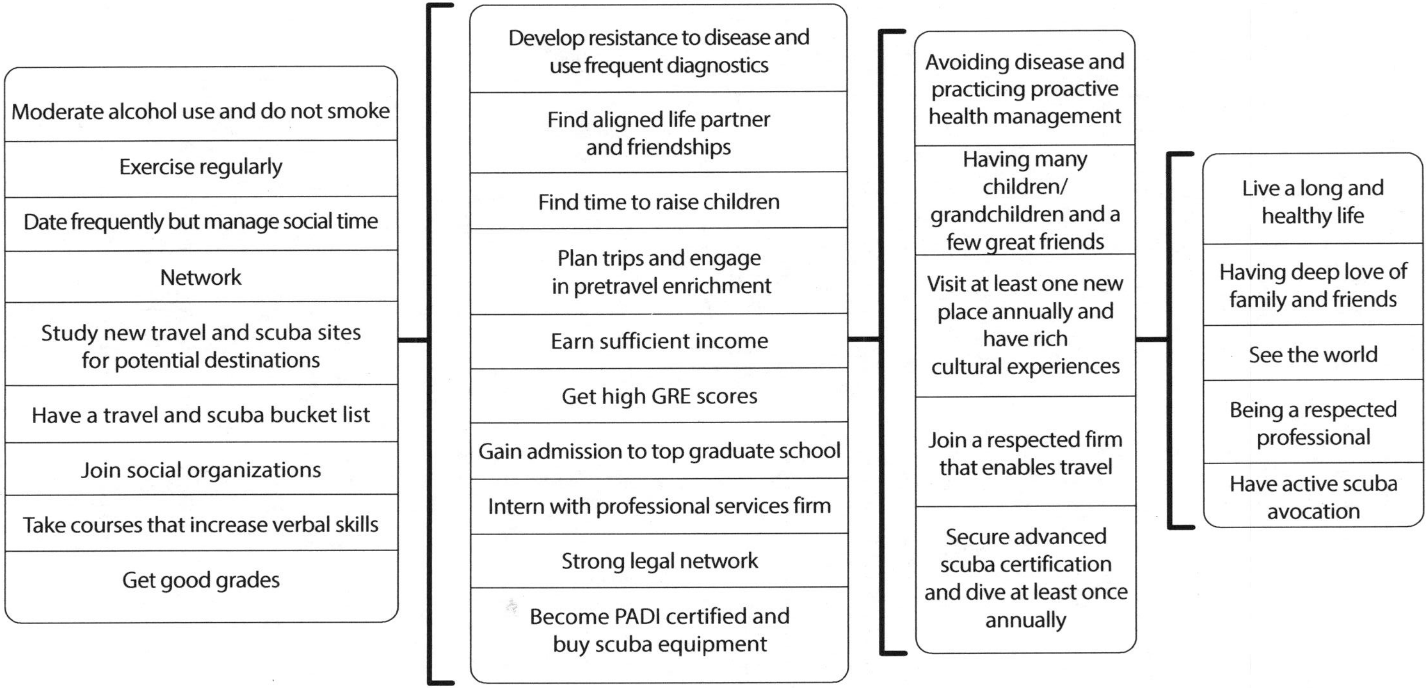

FIGURE 38. Integrated Life Goal Map

Prioritizing across Life Goals

For the most part, we have talked about life goals in isolation. But as in the avocation example, unless we only have one life goal—truly a questionable ideal—we must prioritize across our life goals. Whether we think about it overtly or not, we are constantly making tradeoffs. It is prudent to have a rough idea of key things we want to accomplish and then plan for that time. To do so, it helps to create an integrated life goal map, such as the one shown in figure 38. In this figure, you will see simplified and integrated maps for Will.

What can we learn from putting these maps together? First, while it is easier to map each life goal separately at first, when combined, the tradeoffs and challenges of managing a plan to achieve them become more apparent. Second, some lighthouse goals will also support other lighthouse goals—an ideal situation—such as the travel and scuba example described earlier. Finally, while not a perfect mapping against one's life timeline, it helps to see how various lighthouse goals and drivers may be competing for time at different life stages. This will help when we develop a working life plan.

In this map you can see some synergy between diving and travel. But there is also some synergy between career travel and hobby travel as well, as this individual has picked a career that has enabled him to travel a good deal with organizations that are flexible about his extending those trips for personal travel, including scuba.

One challenge that worried Will when looking at this life map was his health. While he worked out regularly at a gym early in his career, extensive travel would potentially challenge his health life goal. To counteract the risk of becoming sedentary and eating too much while traveling, he reasoned that running would be a good aerobic sport to accompany his travel. With only a pair of shoes and light clothing, he would be ready to run almost anywhere around the world. He sought hotels that had exercise equipment, but running nearly daily was his antidote for stress, variable diet, and jet lag.

FIGURE 39. Life Goals Flow Map

Actions	Drivers	Lighthouse Goals	Life Goals

Another challenge was family. How could he develop strong social relationships while traveling and working in a demanding career role? Part of the answer became finding a spouse who matched him well, so that they could experience travel together when possible, work out together, and share some similar avocations. In this case, his spouse was also a scuba diver, allowing them to share that time together.

But he did have to work hard to manage other friendships and family relationships that would have faded without constant attention. Many of his family members lived far from him. He decided that he needed to make a strong effort to fly out to see family fairly often. He was fortunate in that his business also called for travel to locations close to his parents and other family members, allowing him at least short visits. This, combined with social networks, inexpensive data plans, and e-mail, enabled him to stay closer to many of his best friends over the years.

MAPPING YOUR LIFE GOALS

Take a moment now to convert the life goals, lighthouse goals, success drivers, and actions that you completed earlier (fig. 30) into a life map. Figure 39 provides an open space with headers for the categories that should flow from right to left.

TEST YOUR LIFE GOAL MAP

When you have completed the map, use the worksheet in figure 39 to test your plan and its practicality.

Testing Your Life Map and Assumptions

1. Is there a good cause-effect relationship among the drivers on the left, the lighthouse goals in the middle, and your life goal on the right?
2. Where are possible overlaps or opportunities to combine lighthouse goals or drivers across different life goals?

3. What are some of the potential risks of trying to manage the various lighthouse goals or drivers? Are there likely to be time crunches at certain stages? For example, in the integrated map we discussed a moment ago, would it be practical to be studying for the bar exam, traveling, and getting PADI certified in the same interval? What are some of these risks in your map?
4. Is the plan realistic? Does it seem practical and does it capture your major priorities?
5. What could go wrong? What might prevent you from achieving the path you have just outlined?
6. If you had to make tradeoffs, which life goal or parts of life goals might be reduced or eliminated? What are you prepared to change?

In the next chapter, we will think about how to measure and track your progress.

10

Measuring Your Personal Scorecard

You can't manage what you can't measure.

—Peter Drucker

We measure ourselves every day, sometimes consciously, other times indirectly or unconsciously. Returning to the Olympians I talked about earlier in this book, some of these athletes have clear, objective measures of time or distance; others are judged by more subjective measures, such as judges' opinions of how well they performed. And they track intermediate goals such as earlier races or trials or personal bests, even when not competing in a tournament.

In addition, most of them have drivers that they believe will help them train effectively to meet their goals. Weight goals are a case in point. For weightlifters, it may mean putting on more pounds. For the marathoner, it may mean fewer pounds, but with more muscle, combined with greater stamina. Furthermore, all pounds are not alike. For many athletes, muscle weight is more important than fat weight.

Diets play a crucial role as well. Most athletes have strict regimens of eating that will enable them to build the right strength or stamina and stay healthy while taking the body to its limits. This means obtaining a certain number of calories, vitamins, and other ingredients to help them develop the right way. They also have certain sleep regimens, allowing them to recharge the body in the right way. Marathoners load with carbohydrates before a race and consume protein on a different time schedule, all focused on having the right energy to burn when it really counts.

TYPES OF MEASURES

Regardless of your life goals, there should be clear indicators that show whether you are on track. You can use both objective and subjective measures, as both are appropriate in certain situations, and both can help you track your progress along your life path. While subjective ratings may feel soft, they can be useful against internal or external standards, allowing you to track where you are against your goals.

For example, when you go to a health care professional these days, he or she will often ask you what your pain level is on a scale of zero (none) to ten (worst possible). While that may feel subjective, it is helpful to him or her (and to insurers) in assessing where you are today and how effective treatments have been in reducing your pain.

There are no objective standards for pain. Your doctor cannot tell you how much pain you have based on the symptoms you display. Some people have a low tolerance for pain while others can stand much higher levels. What is a seven for one person may be a ten for another. Only you can judge your relative level of pain. The same is true for fulfillment. It doesn't matter if someone else agrees or disagrees; fulfillment is in the eye of the beholder.

Objective measures provide a specific metric or number that multiple people can verify, such as the length of a football field, your height and weight, or the speed of your car. Attractiveness, on the other hand, often includes objective factors such as height, weight, or dimples, but it also includes more subjective factors such as smile, charisma, and presence, which can only be assessed through the lens of the observer.

A few years back, I was sitting with two female friends who were commenting on several males in the room. Looking at the same male, one said he was incredibly attractive while the other shrugged her shoulder, saying he "did not move her." They were both looking at the objective characteristics (height, weight, hair color), but they used their own attractiveness lens to judge the subjective factors.

Measuring Goals, Drivers, and Actions

I am often asked if one needs different types of measures for life goals than lighthouse goals or drivers. The answer is often no. In some cases, they could be the same. Let's take a look back at the life goals in our legal example. To that life goal of becoming a judge, we will add something this particular judge wanted—self- and community recognition that she made a difference. Some of the measures will be obvious; others will not be.

Start at the top of figure 40, becoming fulfilled from acknowledgment that you have made a difference as a judge. Being honored in your profession could be simply a self-rating of how well you feel you have done. Rate yourself on a scale of one to ten, with ten being perfection against your own standards, which ultimately will be most important to your personal fulfillment.

Many people with life goals also seek feedback from others to affirm their goals. When Sir Edmund Hillary was the first known explorer to scale Mount Everest, it was clearly an exhilarating moment—the achievement of a life quest to be savored. But even in that context, he reported, "While on top of Everest, I looked across the valley towards the great peak Makalu and mentally worked out a route about how it could be climbed. It showed me that even though I was standing on top of the world, it wasn't the end of everything. I was still looking beyond to other interesting challenges."

He saw climbing Everest as part of a broader life quest, saying, "I have enjoyed great satisfaction from my climb of Everest and my trips to the poles. But there's no doubt, either, that my most worthwhile things have been the building of schools and medical clinics. That has given me more satisfaction than a footprint on a mountain."[3]

Although difficult to do, he could have perhaps achieved climbing Everest and kept the ascent personal, but it was important to Hillary to share that with the world. He also thrived on the world sharing his accomplishments. Many people value feedback from others regarding accomplishments that are more public or from relationships that are crucial to personal fulfillment.

FIGURE 40. Measuring Life Goal Fulfillment

Life Goals	Self-Rating (1–10)	Feedback from Others
Become a judge, having made a difference		
Lighthouse Goals	Self-Rating (1–10)	Feedback from Others
Practice in name law firm		
Law degree		
Drivers	Self-Rating (1–10)	Feedback from Others
High LSAT scores		
Admission to top law school		
Intern with name judge		
Strong legal network		
Actions	Self-Rating (1–10)	Feedback from Others
Stay healthy		
Limit social time		
High grades		
Take courses to increase verbal skills		
Network with regional legal professionals		

As I mentioned earlier, my father-in-law was a perfectionist regarding jewelry and diamonds and was a tough judge of his own work. His own standards were far higher than those of his customers. His partner, Bob, however, was also a tough judge of quality and workmanship. My father-in-law valued Bob's judgment highly, and he would take Bob's feedback to heart far more often than the feedback of a less qualified judge, such as the average customer. Receiving recognition or accolades from peers is powerful. This might include such measures as these:

- being inducted as a fellow in a professional society
- receiving awards from professional, avocational, or community organizations that you value
- receiving a collection of recommendation letters from colleagues, peers, or clients
- achieving tenure at a university
- being invited to speak to professional or community groups
- getting a mention of your contribution at an employee event (Many companies such as Bayada Home Health Care have annual events in which employees with particular achievements over the past year are recognized.)

If your map is balanced and complete, you will likely have some of these types of things already in your lighthouse goals or drivers, providing feedback along the way that you are either on or off track.

For our judge-to-be, given the value she placed on making a difference, she could list accomplishments that would indicate she was achieving her goal—named to a special board, recognized for key court decisions, honored or awarded by the legal profession, asked to speak at events, or given community recognitions. She might tally up a list of such outcomes against some hypothetical setbacks, such as a controversial judgment with bad press. In the end, it is up to her to honestly "judge" her own merits against the "evidence" she has gathered on her impact in the profession.

Let's move from the legal profession to my practical aunt Marie, who in many ways was a natural leader. While she would have never described herself using those words, a major part of her life goals was being a leader and role model for others. She was a dedicated worker for the phone company, moving to middle managerial roles. She loved to organize and develop people. This love took place in many parts of her life. At work, she was promoted to manager with a chance to train young people and to organize teams. She had stellar organizing skills and put those to work to help the group hit their targets and succeed.

She also loved bowling, but not just bowling by herself; she loved the team experience and played on several teams each week and helped organize the bowling leagues. She got a thrill out of receiving awards, giving honors, and praising others. And in our family, she was the matriarch of organizing. She was the person who put together family reunions, planned them exquisitely, and kept in touch with extended family members whom we rarely saw. She was a connector and an enabler, and in doing so found incredible fulfillment.

How did she measure this? At work, it was her performance review and the scores her team achieved in the telephone company—a well-measured group. At bowling, it was her personal scores, her team scores, and trophies. In the family, it was the personal appreciation that she received from friends and family. While she probably didn't record all the phone calls she got thanking her for organizing this or that, I'll bet she knew from the frequency of positive feedback that she was the most connected person in our family. She knew she was serving an important, and fulfilling, role.

A Turn in the Road

A number of colleagues that I know were en route to tenure at a university or school but for one reason or another didn't make it. This clearly was an indicator that they were off track in reaching their lifetime academic career goals. However, one professor that I know had a passion for teaching; research was not his primary thing. Had he been given tenure by his first university, he may not have been fulfilled because he would have been under constant pressure to conduct and publish research. Instead, he moved to a university that valued teaching as a primary activity, and he felt far more fulfilled.

Another colleague saw being turned down for tenure as an opportunity to reexamine his life and career. What else did he like? What did he like most about what he did at the university? For him, it was doing research, but he liked applied research that he could see creating a difference for individuals and organizations. And he didn't like the pressure to obtain grants, nor was he enamored of university bureaucracy. He thought he would experiment with working for an applied research organization. He was an immediate success.

YOUR EARLY WARNING INDICATORS

As with goals, you can take a similar approach to measuring your actions and drivers. Some of the subjective judgment measures will come from your own heart, while others are more objective—even verifiable—by others. For our aspiring judge, the action of staying healthy is best known to her and her physician, but others can witness weigh gains, loss of stamina, or sickness.

Getting good grades is a semipublic activity. Certainly your school and those who ask for transcripts will know. And taking courses to increase verbal skills, another action on our judge's list, is easy to count. A more subjective area is social time. Limiting social time to focus on school is more likely measured by its impact on other things, such as your study habits or grades.

Drivers for our judge included admission to a top law school and good LSAT scores. Those are straightforward to measure. You can discover the LSAT requirements for good law schools, you know where you got accepted, and it is clear whether you graduated. Achieving a good internship is also easily measured. In contrast, building a strong legal network is more subjective. Having a thousand "friends" is different than having twenty friends.

In the legal world, as in many other places, the people you know will be important to accessing opportunities. So our aspiring judge will need to think carefully about how many of the "right" people she has in her network. She will probably become more savvy in this regard by actively networking (an action) and learning what a critical sized network should be—asking mentors or advisors for helpful strategies and key people to reach out to—and settling on a manageable number to target.

The most important part of the measurement process is having a tool that you will use to assess where you are on your journey to your goals. Figures 41 and 42 provide a set of examples for you to review to help you think about your own measures. Some will simply be the completion of something, such as getting into law school or getting a job that you desire. For others that are more subjective, they can be scored on a relative scale of one to ten, with ten representing perfect achievement of the target and one representing a complete miss. You can use this for things that you want to improve from "weak or uncompetitive" to "strong or competitive."

For Bridget, the "Sample Measurement Plan for Seeing the World and Scuba Avocation" template (fig. 43) was helpful. To step up this area and meet her life goals, her decision to start with the consulting firm afforded her the financial means to begin doing some travel. Her income would be much higher, and if she planned well, she could combine some personal travel with her business travel. She wanted to become a better planner and began studying guide books and also looking for more exotic locations than she had ventured to before. She created a bucket list of destinations that she would like to see in her lifetime, realizing that her circumstances might change with a spouse and family. The exercise also provided her the insight that whoever she married would have to be travel friendly. She hoped she might meet such a person on one of her newly planned trips.

Figure 44 is a blank template for you to use to score where you are on your life goals, lighthouse goals, and today's actions.

FIGURE 41. Live a Long and Healthy Life

Life Plan	Measures	Score Today	Target Tomorrow
	Enter specific measure you are using; or, enter "Rating" and 1–10 in the Score Today column	*For objective measures, enter actual number (e.g., grade/weight); for "Rating," enter 1 (low) to 10 (high)*	*List your target for objective measures and desired rating for subjective ones*
Life Goals	Measures	Score Today	Target Tomorrow
Live a long and healthy life	Rating	5	7
Lighthouse Goals	Measures	Score Today	Target Tomorrow
Avoid diseases	Rating	6	8
Proactive health management	Rating	3	5
Success Drivers	Measures	Score Today	Target Tomorrow
Resist disease	Rating	6	8
Seek frequent diagnostics	Rating	2	5
Actions	Measures	Score Today	Target Tomorrow
No smoking	Times smoking per week	10	5
Moderate alcohol	Times drinking per week	5	0
Seven hours of sleep	Hours of sleep per day	5	7
Exercise five times per week	Number of times per week	0	5
Annual physical	Number of physicals per year	0	1
Regular dental cleanings	Number of dental cleanings per year	0	2

FIGURE 42. Sample Measurement Plan for Becoming a Judge

Life Plan	Measures	Score Today	Target Tomorrow
	Enter specific measure you are using; or, enter "Rating" and 1–10 in the Score Today column	*For objective measures, enter actual number (e.g., grade/weight); for "Rating," enter 1 (low) to 10 (high)*	*List your target for objective measures and desired rating for subjective ones*
Life Goals	Measures	Score Today	Target Tomorrow
Becoming a judge	Rating	No	Yes
Lighthouse Goals	Measures	Score Today	Target Tomorrow
Practice in name law firm	Rating	No	Yes
Law degree	Rating	No	Yes
Success Drivers	Measures	Score Today	Target Tomorrow
Get high LSAT scores	Rating	160	170
Admission to top law school	Number of top law schools admitted into	Not yet	Acceptance
Internship with well-known judge	Number of interviews with judges	2	5
Create a strong legal network	Number of connections	15 attorneys	50 attorneys
Actions	Measures	Score Today	Target Tomorrow
Stay healthy	Rating	4	6
Limit social time	Rating	20 hrs./wk.	10 hrs./wk.
Get high grades	Grade in classes	B average	A– average
Take courses that increase verbal skill	Grade in these courses	C	A
Network with regional legal professionals	Number of connections	3	20

FIGURE 43. Sample Measurement Plan for Seeing the World and Scuba Avocation

Life Plan	Measures	Score Today	Target Tomorrow
	Enter specific measure you are using; or, enter "Rating" and 1–10 in the Score Today column	*For objective measures, enter actual number (e.g., grade/weight); for "Rating," enter 1 (low) to 10 (high)*	*List your target for objective measures and desired rating for subjective ones*
Life Goals	Measures	Score Today	Target Tomorrow
See the world	Number of countries traveled to	3	10
Have active scuba avocation	Dives per year	8	30
Lighthouse Goals	Measures	Score Today	Target Tomorrow
Visit at least one new place annually	Number of places visited annually	1	1
Have rich cultural experiences	Rating	2	7
Secure advanced certification	Advanced open water certification/ Nitrox certifications	Nitrox: Yes Advanced open: No	Nitrox and advanced open water certified
Success Drivers	Measures	Score Today	Target Tomorrow
Earn sufficient income	Income earned per year	$60,000	$90,000
Plan like a travel agent	Rating	3	6
Become PADI (basic) certified	Receive certification	Yes	Future maintain certification
Buy scuba equipment	Rating	2 = Rent today	10 = Own top of the line
Actions	Measures	Score Today	Target Tomorrow
Study world sites	Rating	5	8
Have a travel and scuba bucket list	Number of identified sites	10	25
Take diving classes	Number	1	2
Network with divers	Number of scuba connections	3	15

FIGURE 44. Measures for Your Goals

Life Plan	Measures	Score Today	Target Tomorrow
	Enter specific measure you are using; or, enter "Rating" and 1–10 in the Score Today column	*For objective measures, enter actual number (e.g., grade/weight); for "Rating," enter 1 (low) to 10 (high)*	*List your target for objective measures and desired rating for subjective ones*
Life Goals	Measures	Score Today	Target Tomorrow
Lighthouse Goals	Measures	Score Today	Target Tomorrow

Life Plan	*Measures*	*Score Today*	*Target Tomorrow*
	Enter specific measure you are using; or, enter "Rating" and 1–10 in the Score Today column	*For objective measures, enter actual number (e.g., grade/weight); for "Rating," enter 1 (low) to 10 (high)*	*List your target for objective measures and desired rating for subjective ones*
Success Drivers	Measures	Score Today	Target Tomorrow
Actions	Measures	Score Today	Target Tomorrow

11

Finishing Your Plan

*Planning is bringing the future into the present
so that you can do something about it now.*

—Alan Lakein

While we can and should dream of what will bring us fulfillment, we also must be practical in finding a path to achieve those dreams—one that stretches us but does not require impossible assumptions. Getting a bachelor's degree, a law degree, and a medical degree are all possible but it would not be practical to do so at the same time. Joe Montana, one of the greatest American football quarterbacks of all time, could have also been a basketball star. Montana was offered a basketball scholarship to North Carolina State University but chose to go to Notre Dame and focus on football.[1]

Bo Jackson tried to do both; he was a college superstar in baseball and football. In fact, he was such a superstar that he accepted professional roles with both the Kansas City Royals baseball team and the Los Angeles Raiders football team. Although the teams tried to accommodate his schedules, he soon found that the punishing nature of football on his body would certainly limit his career in baseball, so he dropped professional football and concentrated on baseball.[2]

Could Bo Jackson have known when he was ten that he would face this choice? Unlikely! However, with a life plan, it is possible to pursue paths that provide you with multiple choices. In other words, some activities will assure that you still can choose multiple paths in the future. I will provide an example from my own life. I'm not sure that this is a recommended model, but it demonstrates the point. I began college in electrical engineering (EE), taking the core courses required. When I decided in my third semester that I didn't prefer EE, I was able to switch to industrial engineering with almost no loss of time or effort.

Still, I was unsure of engineering, beginning to think more about business or some way to combine my interests in math with people issues. I began to take courses in accounting, labor relations, and psychology that would enable me to still have choices depending on how well I liked these different fields. I tentatively switched to accounting but realized that it did not have enough of the people element.

Eventually—five semesters into college—I found a curriculum of industrial psychology that combined elements of industrial engineering, industrial relations, and psychology in a way that felt exciting. Despite only having three semesters remaining in a standard curriculum, I was now able to concentrate in that field and complete my bachelor's degree in the standard four years. However, I had tried four different directions during that time. What enabled me to experiment was a rough plan that continued my education in courses that were foundational for a variety of different directions, using what I learned about myself, as well as the course content, to shape my final decision.

While this description sounds wonderfully insightful in hindsight, it was less so during that period. However, it could have been more effective if I had applied the principles of this book, which I have learned since. One's career, love interests, and hobbies should not be a matter of luck but rather honed to one's unique nature. I was lucky to hit the right path with some foresight, but I also watched friends crash and burn during that same period because they bet the ranch on electrical engineering or literature and painted themselves into a corner, either running out of money for college or running out of energy.

The critical point is that there is great value in having a life plan, but it needs to be flexible to account for changes in interests, life events, and the world at large.

BUILDING A SOUND LIFE PLAN

It is helpful to consider one's interests, goals, and opportunities in a more thoughtful way than I did at the early stages of my life. In my high school, career coaching was abysmal. The wrestling coach was the career counselor; he was a great wrestling coach, but my experiences with him as a career counselor (when he was available) left something to be desired. I have met many other friends who have had similar experiences. Applying to an engineering college was a bit like throwing a dart and hoping I would hit the bull's-eye.

However, my story contains an important lesson: It is never too late to adjust. Life will present many turns and challenges, and planning will help you adapt to the circumstances—not predict perfectly what you will do. Despite better career coaches, I still had friends in my college who realized that engineering or accounting was not for them. Fortunately, my college had a good psychological testing program that enabled students to reassess their goals, interests, and competencies and make course corrections.

One of my reasons for writing this book is to enable others to reach these stages sooner than I did—to think about fulfillment earlier in one's life. A good plan will not only include life goals, lighthouse goals, and drivers but activities that will be necessary to reach those goals. Transcribing your life map into this plan will help put everything into perspective. On the far right are your life goals, with lighthouse goals, drivers, and actions in different columns. The "right" actions today will enable you to successfully implement those drivers.

Figure 45 provides a sample for the goal of becoming a successful entrepreneur. For example, if you want to be a successful entrepreneur, you have to start a business (lighthouse goal). To do that with the greatest success, you will need to test ideas in a safe environment, create a business plan, and find funding (success drivers). That may mean starting today to think about what you really know—what's your passion—and then booking up on that area of interest. Reading about other entrepreneurial successes and failures will often help avert early disaster. Better yet, talk to some entrepreneurs.

FIGURE 45. Draft Plan for Successful Entrepreneur

Actions	Drivers	Lighthouse Goals	Life Goals
Take time to think about what your passion is	Test out business concepts in safe environment	Start a business	Successful entrepreneur
Talk to entrepreneurs to learn more about their businesses—and their lives	Create a business plan		
Talk to people in your life to determine whether they will support your endeavor	Secure funding for new venture		
Find stories in books, magazines, and newspapers about entrepreneurial ventures			
Take some business or innovation classes			
Realistically assess what you will have to sacrifice in other sectors of your life to be successful			

Next, what kind of support will you have? If you have a spouse, will he or she be supportive in a variety of ways—financially, mentally, and emotionally? You will also need to know about how a business operates, so business or entrepreneurial courses may help. Finally, what are you willing to sacrifice in other aspects of your life to be successful as an entrepreneur? I have known many aspiring entrepreneurs who don't have the risk tolerance to stay the course when difficult times occur—and they often will. Or, they are not willing to give up softball games, or they expect to work forty hours a week when a growing business needs sixty hours or more of their time. This kind of thinking will help you plot your course, with a greater likelihood of being successful at what you ultimately decide you want to do.

Perhaps another life goal is seeing the world, and that requires getting started early. You will need to take actions today—studying exciting places to visit, talking with other travelers and travel agents, finding a job that enables you to travel sufficiently and provides enough income to take trips, and ensuring that your other key relationships will be supportive of your travel.

And while travel may be a good counterbalance to the stresses of being an entrepreneur, you may have to sacrifice travel at certain stages of starting and running a business. In some businesses, it may be impossible to have both of those goals. My auto mechanic friend, whom I described earlier in this book, works six days a week to make the business successful. He takes trips periodically, but it would have been unrealistic for him to have a life goal of travel. The two simply are not compatible in his current business configuration. Perhaps if he had grown the business from the family operation it has been to a larger enterprise, he might have reached a point where he had other people running the business's day-to-day activities, allowing him the luxury of more travel.

MARISA'S SCORECARD

At the beginning of this book, I shared the story of Marisa, who suddenly discovered she was afflicted with stage-four pancreatic cancer. She immediately refocused her life goals to staying alive, shedding all other distractions in her life. Marisa used the balanced scorecard and planning methods that I have described for her battle, resulting in the goals, drivers, and actions in figure 46. Her unitary life goal at this point was getting and staying well. If she didn't, nothing else would matter. Her lighthouse goals were progressive milestones toward recovery, which would lead to remission. Her drivers included hiring the best advisors and

FIGURE 46. Life Goal Mapping for Healing from Pancreatic Cancer

Actions	Success Drivers	Lighthouse Goals	Life Goal
Take leave of absence from work	Take charge—be CEO of my life	Progressive improvement—key milestones	Getting and staying well
Create vision and daily visualizations			
Explore energy, healing, acupuncture, and health workshops	Healthy/ happy lifestyle		
Start anticancer diet, green drinks, and supplements			
Exercise daily			
Hire top oncologist who believes I can get well	Hire top experts	Cancer in remission	
Embrace chemotherapy	Medical treatment		

creating a healthy lifestyle, supported by a variety of key actions, such as adopting an anticancer diet, interviewing oncologists to be on her team, exercising daily, and taking workshops on healing.

After fighting and winning a life-threatening battle, Marisa felt transformed. She then took stock of where she was in life, and in addition to staying cancer-free, she set a revised life goal of "making a difference to others facing life-threatening diagnoses." She set a lighthouse goal of seeing other patients succeed, drivers such as getting the word out in media and becoming an expert coach, and actions that included writing articles and running workshops (see fig. 47).

Think about activities and competencies that may be important to successfully reaching your drivers or lighthouse goals. Begin listing them, keeping in mind the eighty-twenty rule, which says that 20 percent of the time we spend on something is likely to deliver 80 percent of the value. What are the two to four most important things that will allow you to hit your drivers or lighthouse goals?

FIGURE 47. Life Goal Map for Making a Difference to Others Facing Life-Threatening Diagnoses

Actions	Success Drivers	Lighthouse Goals	Life Goal
Revisit vision and daily visualizations	Maintain healthy/happy lifestyle	Cancer in remission; pronounced cured	Staying well Making a difference for people facing life-threatening diagnoses
Exercise daily Eat healthy diet			
Manage energy	Become expert in healing		
Conduct ongoing workshops/ support groups	Connect with patients facing difficult situations		
Share story/ write about experience Say "yes" to TV appearances/ press requests	Appear in print/media	Help patients find the way	

A SUCCESSFUL PLAN

A successful plan will have several elements:

- desired outcome
- clear and specific actions or activities
- timetable for accomplishing the actions
- evaluation tool
- revision of the plan as needed

These five steps will help you draft a solid plan. Let's take a look at each element.

DESIRED OUTCOMES. Desired outcomes are the results you hope to achieve if the actions and activities are successful: a law degree, a job, a master mechanic, a competitive snowboarder. Be specific.

CLEAR AND SPECIFIC ACTIONS OR ACTIVITIES. It is helpful to make sure that your actions or activities are clear and specific. For example, taking a course in political science and being active in a debate or speaking club are clear. Becoming a better communicator or taking relevant courses is too vague.

TIMETABLE. Actions or activities are only relevant if performed in a specific timeframe. For example, studying for a law exam three years early may be of little help if you don't take the exam soon. If you want to prepare for a piano recital, you want to peak at the right time. It will not help if you start practicing a concerto too early or too late.

Timetables also help you sequence activities so that you are not overloaded in one period and inactive in another. A friend of mine was taking a marketing curriculum at the local college and took four courses at once, trying to get through the program quickly. Her plan backfired because it was too much at one time. She had to drop two courses and did not do well in the others. It hurt her GPA, and in the end she had to take two of the courses again.

EVALUATION. Plans without evaluations are useless. How will you know if your plans worked? A quantitative evaluation may provide some precise numbers, but a qualitative one may provide more depth of understanding. For example, if you take courses with the plan of getting a 3.5 GPA to get into grad school, you will know whether you hit that mark. If you have eight courses to go, you will need an A in four and a B in four, for example, to hit the target if you are already at a 3.5. However, a qualitative evaluation may help you understand how well you are learning the course material.

Qualitative judgments can be valuable in other ways as well. You took a yoga class to feel relaxed; did it work? Perhaps ask yourself, on a scale of one to ten, how relaxed you feel. If you are still stressed, perhaps massage or exercise might be a better activity. In this case, your judgment is most important.

Another example of evaluation is garnered from your stake-holders: family, friends, and colleagues. Let's say that you are thinking about law or public relations as a vocation. You decide to take a communication course to become a better speaker and communicator. During the course or at the end, it might be help-ful to ask friends or colleagues, "Do you think I am communicat-ing better?"

REVISION. All plans need revisions. The world is constantly chang-ing, and even our best-laid plans are subject to adjustment to make them relevant to new information or circumstances. After you have implemented actions or activities in your specified timetable and have evaluated the impact of them, you may want to adjust your plan. Perhaps the actions were less effective than you had hoped. The prep course did not raise your test scores, for example. Or the courses at the community college did little to improve your GPA. Perhaps it is time for some soul searching. Were there other actions or activities that you passed over that might have been more effective?

If you have exhausted all of the actions outlined in your plan, you might need to decide that your current goal is not worth the effort, generate some new actions, change your drivers or lighthouse goals, or look for help from others in your network who might provide you with new ideas or actions. You might also need to revise your plan due to unexpected circumstances. For example, let's say you had dreamed of becoming a professional basketball player and had the necessary skills to do it. However, due to an unexpected injury, you can no longer play. What changes must you then make to your life plan? Is there a plan B? Might you focus on becoming a coach or a personal trainer?

PLANS ARE NOT FOREVER

"While being planful, be willing to ad lib. Life presents unexpected opportunities, and if your nose is too close to the grindstone, you're likely to miss them." That's sage advice from Howard Winkler, retired human resource leader from Georgia Power and former chair of the HR Certification Institute.

If you have developed strong values and perhaps a strong vision of your life goals, your path can be molded in different ways to get to the end within your values. One acquaintance of mine believed the way to get money was to marry a woman from a wealthy family. He was constantly trying to find the "right" girl to marry so that his road to riches was shortened. At the same time, he desperately wanted a quality relationship. Many of his relationships were short-lived because he could not reconcile his values with his monetary goal. He would have to change either his values or his goal.

Another acquaintance had planned for a career in biology. He was one of the smartest people I knew. He planned his path carefully and got a PhD from one of the best universities in North America. He interned with a large corporation with a great reputation. However, he struggled to find fulfilling research roles. He always seemed to be chasing research money or tenured slots. He kept working at this but became more and more cynical about the system and how it didn't reward truly committed people.

At some point, I think he would have been better to turn his attention and incredible mind to an adjacent field because his relentless pursuit of this life goal was no longer leading to his life fulfillment. This pursuit also took a toll on other parts of his life because his spouse—who had been very supportive over many years—was beginning to show signs of frustration. He became a sort of Don Quixote in search of an impossible dream.

Take your plan and use it for what it is—a time capsule for what is best for you now. However, you should view it as a temporal plan to be adjusted, updated, and changed continually throughout your life. Because I love travel so much, a travel analogy comes to mind. If your goal is to see the world, you should relish your first trip to a new continent. But you should not view that trip as the end—it's only part of the journey.

Take some time now to reflect on your life plan. What actions would be most important for you at this stage of your life? Can you find ways to combine actions that will help you reach several goals?

BALANCE SHORT AND LONG TERM

Although this book is focused on long-term life goals, life is about enjoying the journey, if we can manage it. I will be the first person to say that this book is not about achieving some distant life goal and not being fulfilled along the way. All deferred gratification and no short-term enjoyment leads to an austere life that may not keep you motivated to continue.

To maintain balance, you need some clear long-term goals as a framework. With that framework, you can build in short-term goals and actions that will bring fulfillment throughout your life. One cannot defer building a wonderful friendship network until the age of sixty. One cannot expect to be a virtuoso piano player and not bother to start until retirement.

WHAT ABOUT BRIDGET?

Bridget wrestled with two big issues: finding a spouse that she could build a family with and choosing the "right" career. Also, a secondary life goal was "seeing the world." After working through this thinking, she realized that she needed to devote the right amount of time to social activities that would enable her to connect with a potential future spouse. However, she should not overdo it while finishing her degree.

You may remember that she was not sure whether she should work for a big corporation, a small consulting firm, or start a business with her brother. After working through this process, she realized that she didn't have the risk tolerance for a business start-up, nor would it provide time to travel. Furthermore, the large corporation offered her a more predictable schedule but would damage her ability to travel, so she started down a path of working for a consulting firm in which she would get to travel and meet interesting spousal candidates at the firm or while traveling. Perhaps when she was ready to have children, she would move to a larger corporation with a more predictable schedule and stronger benefits for a family.

Life Is Short: Do the Important Things While You Can

It is not wrong to be totally immersed in one's profession. One colleague that I know in Europe was totally immersed in his profession for more than twenty-five years before finding a steady girlfriend, who later became his wife. Today, he combines family and travel in a way that really fulfills him. It is not for us to judge whether he was fulfilled during those workaholic years. However, the purpose of writing this book is to enable you to plan such actions consciously, not allowing them to happen as chance.

I was preparing to take a trip across the Southwestern United States—an incredibly beautiful area with majestic mountains, the Grand Canyon, desert life, and intriguing Native American villages. As I was telling another colleague who was exceedingly successful in his career about the trip, he stopped me suddenly and said, "You are good to be doing that. You are so lucky!" I was taken aback because he was certainly someone who had the money to do so if he desired. So I asked him what he meant.

He proceeded to tell me about missing so many years of travel and enjoyment with his family, instead enduring twenty-plus years of stress and suffering a heart attack in his forties. I'd had no idea. He always put on a good game face at professional meetings. Now he has the money to live in a great retirement community, play golf four days a week, and travel, but he related to me that he had missed so much along the way.

Life is about making choices and having no regrets. It is my hope that this type of planning and thinking will enable you to embark on a journey—regardless of where you start—that has no regrets.

PART IV

THE ART OF FULFILLMENT

Life Lessons from the Fulfilled

As I said early in this book, fulfillment is about not only planning for the future but also learning from the wisdom of others and applying it to your own life. One group we studied included approximately one hundred seasoned individuals who had multiple jobs, had lived in different locations over the years, and had at least the outward appearance of success. Some had multiple marriages, with and without kids. We also talked to single dads and moms.

But once we dug below the surface, we found a high degree of variability in levels of fulfillment. We found a modest number who were highly fulfilled, many who were partially fulfilled, and still others with very little fulfillment. However, most had learned something along the way—lessons they would gladly pass along to a protégé, a friend, or a loved one.

In this section, I selected the ten most frequent strategies for achieving success and long-term fulfillment that we learned from our interviewees. For a description of other strategies not included in this chapter, see the website http://www.wschiemann/com/fulfilled.

Some strategies fit your situation more than others. But our research team never found a highly fulfilled person who did not employ a variety of the strategies described in this section. Not all individuals used these strategies the same way or at the same time, and quite a few learned new strategies over time.

Before reviewing the results of the interviews, we pondered whether these life lessons would be applicable to people of all ages. Interestingly, most of them are. The reality is that many people get started on their path to fulfillment at different times in their lives. Some have lived quite unfulfilling lives only to discover late in life what counts in their quest for fulfillment. Others have enlightened moments in college, in searching for a first job, or perhaps after a stint in their first career or first marriage.

Now that you have a better understanding of what fulfillment means, and the science of preparing and planning for it from the last section of this book, ask yourself how good you are at the art of fulfillment. Do you have street-smart ways to apply the science of fulfillment to real life? The lessons in this section were learned over time to adjust to challenges, overcome setbacks, and leverage opportunities. Quite simply, they represent wisdom from those who have traveled life's paths.

12

Life Lessons

Part I

Every day, you are writing your story.
—Chris Palmer, vice president of Human
Resources Americas, Volvo Cars

This chapter looks at the first five lessons we learned about the art of becoming fulfilled. These lessons are not listed by order of importance or application. However, we do start with an important connection to what you pondered about your life goals in the last section of this book.

LESSON 1: KEEP THE END IN MIND

The most important lesson passed along by our fulfilled panel is to keep focused on the end goal—fulfillment! This book has been about creating goals, drivers, and activities that will lead you to fulfillment.

Remember that we each have the same twenty-four hours in the day. So how are we going to spend that time? If you don't know the goal, any road will get you there. Earlier in life, it may be more difficult—so many paths, opportunities, advisors. It is difficult to ferret out what will bring us fulfillment. For less advantaged individuals, the options may look grim. The challenge may be identifying even one path or finding even one personal advisor who cares.

But keep in mind that research has shown that fulfilled individuals come from all walks of life and backgrounds.[1] Being born with a silver spoon is no guarantee of fulfillment, and being born impoverished may limit opportunities, but many influential leaders, successful people, and fulfilled individuals have come from the ranks of the poor. The one area that most all our panel agreed on is that you cannot be happy, successful, or fulfilled without giving some thought to your future vision and how you might get there. The earlier we can ascertain some meaningful goals, or at least eliminate paths that do not bring fulfillment, the more quickly we can accelerate the road to a life of fulfillment. Most of our panelists shared insights they discovered along the way as they tried different paths.

Bridget, whom we have followed throughout this book, has many choices ahead of her. What helped her was thinking about her true life goals—her North Star—and then dealing with the choices in that context. A huge relief for her was discovering that the immediate choices she faced were not "forever" decisions, as long as they provided a potential path to her endgame. Choosing to work for a consulting firm did not close off future options to reach her life goals; instead, it opened up new channels. Whether she sticks with that career step will be a minor detail when she looks back on her life. It will more likely be viewed as one small step in Bridget's life path that nudged her in the right direction.

Earlier we acknowledged that what fulfills you today may be different than what fulfills you tomorrow. But unless you think about it, you are likely to spend more and more time on actions and decisions that will not lead to your fulfillment.

LESSON 2: NURTURE YOUR BODY

This advice seems obvious. Without a strong body and mind, the rest is naught. When you have been seriously ill in your life, you realize that there is little else if you don't have your health. If you lack energy, stamina, and a clear and relaxed mind or if you are held back by mental or physical pain, it is hard to be innovative, enjoy friends and family, get excited about accomplishing things at work, or get into a special hobby. And yet most humans in the world have experienced or will experience some form of physical setback. Others will deal, or are already dealing, with family members who have physical setbacks.

The question is how good we are at managing our health. Two factors to this lesson are prevention and recovery. The first relates to what elements we can control in our lives. What physical or mental adversities can be avoided? Let's take a look at a few of the major preventive health contributors.

EXERCISE. The evidence is overwhelming today that exercise leads to healthier and longer lives. Exercise can reduce the risk of coronary ailments such as hypertension that can lead to strokes while increasing cardiovascular capacity, with a host of benefits for your overall energy levels and vigor. The National Cancer Institute even says exercise can reduce the risk of developing many types of cancer.[2] Strength exercises increase stamina and the ability to take on physical demands and also reduce injuries. *(Note: Consult a physician before embarking on a new exercise program, especially if you have been sedentary.)*

Many who exercise report psychological benefits as well—more energy, optimism, and feelings of control.[3] Runners and bikers frequently report a "high" that comes with exercise. Marisa Harris, whom we introduced at the beginning of this book, said, "When I run, I find myself more productive in the rest of my life—my job, family, and hobbies." A recent study suggested that a mere five minutes—you read that right: five minutes— of running a day may reduce cardiovascular risks by as much as 45 percent.[4] It takes longer than that to drink your cappuccino!

SMART EATING HABITS. There are hundreds of diet books, food news-letters, blogs, magazines, and even talk shows on food and eating. I won't repeat what most of us have heard, but often that knowledge does not translate to good behaviors. "You are what you eat!" coined by Victor Lindlahr, is not just a slogan.[5]

A friend of mine gave me a helpful tool in my early twenties. I remember Cary sitting on the couch watching Chicago Cubs games with a bag of potato chips. When we put together a pickup game of baseball, Cary could rarely outrun the throw to first base. He stopped riding bicycles with many of us. He had become a couch potato.

I didn't see Cary for a number of years and was shocked to see his lifestyle change. He had slimmed down, ate healthier, and was now a runner. I would never have predicted it. When we talked, he said his renaissance came about during college when he realized that he had to compete with others—for grades, for dates, for friends—and he started to change. When I asked him about the potato chips, he said that he turned the corner when he began picturing what each potato chip was doing in his body as it turned into a glob of gray, gooey fat sticking to him. Cary has used this mental image (and I have stolen it from him) to avoid the habit. One of the key factors that transcends our list of recommendations is control. People who were fulfilled also felt more control in their lives. Having control of food is an important element of health.

PREVENTIVE MEDICAL PRACTICES. The last area of focus for health is preventive medical practices, which range from simple routines such as flossing to prevent tooth decay to regular medical check-ups. A number of our fulfilled people took preventive actions to minimize their chances of medical setbacks. Most of us don't start that way, but it appears that those who live long lives—long enough to provide sage advice—have developed good practices along the way. Most of the panel we interviewed lamented not starting some actions sooner. A man having dental work done asked the dentist which days he could skip flossing. The dentist sagely replied, "On the ones that you don't care about damaging your teeth."

While I am not preaching fanaticism here, there is some value to Benjamin Franklin's adage about an ounce of prevention being worth a pound of cure. Here are a few health-related steps to consider in your own life:

- Have regular medical checkups. These include breast checkups for women and prostate checkups for men. Consult your physician on timing based on your age and family history.
- Create a medical baseline. In order to understand later ailments or problems, consider doing a full medical work-up early in life. Colleges sometimes have relatively inexpensive programs. As I got older and had some problems, I realized that I had no baseline readings taken when I was healthy. One of the things that I have advocated is investing in MRIs, X-rays, and other key diagnostics to get a full picture of the body when one is young. While your insurance company may balk at this, I suggest that it is a good investment. The costs of treating diseases and conditions later in life are staggering and continuing to skyrocket.
- Insist on good diagnostics. As I have sadly discovered in my own life and that of close friends, this is far from the universal practice today. My wife consulted more than ten doctors over a period of three years before her own "Dr. House" correctly diagnosed and treated her inflammatory disease. She had no baseline readings from earlier in her life and suffered because of poor diagnoses. Lyme disease, fibromyalgia, simple arthritis, hormone issues, spinal injury, bone spurs, or calcium deposits were all diagnosed (guessed?) by doctors across four medical systems, including some with prestigious names, but incorrectly! I have gone through a similar process with a persistent cough that has worsened over five years, but visits to five pulmonologists, ENTs, generalists, gastroenterologists, and allergists have been unsuccessful

in diagnosing the cause. Amazing? You bet! And I am not alone; when I reveal our stories to others, they are often met with similar frustrating stories.

- Be diligent. Dietary and medical diligence can help you on the road to fulfillment because medical disabilities almost always diminish your full ability to reach goals and the lifestyle you desire.
- Use prevention techniques. While prevention requires energy and takes time, it usually enables you to live a fuller life, have the energy to work toward your life goals, and have the resilience to overcome setbacks.

A frequent topic among those interviewed was recovering from setbacks, including recovery from physical or mental injuries. It is hard to get up when you are knocked down. When I went to the gym a few months ago, I met a fellow in the therapy pool who I knew worked out frequently. He surprised me by telling me that he just had both knees replaced a few weeks earlier.

I asked, "What are you doing here? Why aren't you home recovering?"

He said, "Home is not the place to recover mentally or physically." He went on to talk about how he has recovered from other setbacks with a similar philosophy. He practically leaped out of the hospital, demanded the best physical therapist in the area, insisted on doing therapy as frequently as possible, asked them to push him as hard as they could, and treated his recovery as his primary life work. He voluntarily came to the gym to swim, which he could do as much as he wanted; it was his way of saying "I'm back" both mentally and physically. He was back on his feet in no time, back to work, and back to life.

Attitude is important, according to the many we interviewed, as well as making recovery a central feature of your life when needed. At the age of twenty-one, Stephen Hawking, the famous mathematician, physicist, and cosmologist, was diagnosed with ALS, or Lou Gehrig's disease. However, he did not let this stop his desires to contribute to the world as he has done; he knew there were tasks he still had to accomplish. In 1963, Hawking was given two years to live. He decided to concentrate on finishing his studies. He went to Cambridge and became a brilliant researcher and professorial fellow, racking up honorary degrees and professional accolades. Despite the odds, he is still alive and has become famous through his research. He is regarded as one of the most brilliant physicists since Einstein.[6]

The key point is to continue nurturing your body. It is your life system in a churning sea of challenges. When you are young, you feel invincible, but most of those we talked to later in life wished that they had been better to their life system.

Lesson 3: Build a Social Network (but Have at Least One Fantastic Friend)

How important are friends? With the surge of social media, it appears that we are more connected than ever before. And yet, as Lon, a millennial, reflects, "I have tons of contacts but only a few good friends." What was interesting is that those we interviewed in every generation said something similar. Extroverts seem to have a far more developed network of contacts than introverts. A few introverts said that they don't participate in Facebook, LinkedIn, and other social media sites and limit their communication to a rather small network. Extroverts on the other hand took pride in how many Facebook friends or LinkedIn connections they had.

While the level of communication varied, it seems that the one factor that makes the biggest difference is having a couple of close friends. Karin joked, "I 'friend' a lot of people on Facebook, but I only really have three friends—true friends." Apparently, those friends are the ones that she goes to for objective feedback about herself.

"Marco said I talk too much. Do you think that is true?"

"I have a new job offer. It pays a lot more than what I am making today, but it seems less social or friendly than my current job. Do you think it is a good move for me?"

Others such as Ralph said that he got out of school, took positions in Europe and Asia for about four years, and everything was riding high. He met his wife during those years. And then the bottom fell out. "My specialization in Japanese language and culture all of a sudden went from high demand to no demand." Ralph became seriously depressed, looking back over twelve years invested in something he loved and that he had bet his career on.

His only true friend—his wife, Martha—got him through that period. She provided both the sympathy to acknowledge his feelings and also the kick to move him on. She convinced him that he had good writing skills and could be an editor. Eventually he began applying for related positions and started with modest jobs that later grew into the role of editor. Japanese culture and philosophy became his serious hobby, while his day job provided income and a sense of accomplishment.

Friends count. Almost every one of our fulfilled interviewees cited having at least one or two great friends. Many of them recounted how those friends were important during transitions in their life—marriages, jobs, or even careers. Some helped during crises with parents or other family members. Most often the help consisted of active listening, providing empathy, and giving the kind of objective feedback that is so difficult to get from others.

If you want to be fulfilled, find and develop a few great friends. I use the term *develop* because a number of our interviewees recounted that they had lost good friends from earlier in their lives due to neglect. They were too busy with family or career or a hobby, and the relationship withered and died. When you have a good friend, or believe you are developing one, make sure you put in the right time and contribution to evolve that relationship. Friendship is a two-way street. The very same characteristics that helped these people—listening, caring, and objective feedback—are also important to give to a friend when they are in need.

While friends count, a note of caution was offered from our fulfilled panelists. If you hang out with people who are disengaged, cynical, and mistrusting, then all of their coaching will lead you down a path to perennial unhappiness. If you hang out with people who are engaged, they can provide realistic counsel on how you can get unstuck. Find them, grow them, and nurture them!

LESSON 4: ALWAYS SEEK THINGS YOU ARE PASSIONATE ABOUT

This was one of the most frequently repeated messages from those who had been around the proverbial block many times. These sages said anything worth doing is worth doing well—with passion. That includes jobs, relationships, hobbies, friends—essentially anything you spend time on.

Now, it is easy to say that in hindsight—and most of these comments were from people looking back over their lives and the lives of others they have watched. On the career front, David P. Campbell said, "Follow your passions . . . do what you are passionate about and forget the money."

When I asked those who said "follow your passions" whether they followed that advice when they were starting out, about one-quarter said yes, almost half said they followed the money, and the rest took a variety of paths that often balanced their passions and their need to support themselves or their family.

Most described having a variety of influencers in their life path. Their friends kibitzed, parents pushed, or a spouse or partner cajoled them toward a job that earned more pay, a position close to home, or something that was safe. But in hindsight, 90 percent of them said that following your passion is the surest way to happiness. Most also admitted that you have to live and find a way to earn enough money to support yourself. The most fulfilled took jobs that fulfilled them personally—not just filled their wallets.

That is not always easy. One of my colleagues knows a young woman who is smart, has a four-year degree, but took what she considered to be a boring job because she has a young daughter and sickly mother whom she needs to support. She feels she cannot stop working to take time to be an apprentice in something she is more passionate about. She and many others live paycheck to paycheck. Many people are in situations that have limited career options because of other needs in their lives. However, numerous people we interviewed had great challenges earlier in their lives. They often talked about creating a vision of how their life would change, taking small steps such as evening college courses or getting their GED to move their life forward, aiming to do jobs that they could be more engaged with, and bit by bit measuring how things were improving—even if slowly at first.

Some cannot make it despite earnest effort because the situations around them are too onerous. But thinking about passion and a future vision, and taking whatever actions they can along that path, provides some opportunity for change. Regardless of your situation, you can always dream. Not all dreams will come true, but without dreams, none will come true.

Passion is not restricted to work. For many, a passion is associated with relationships. Many of our interviewees had been divorced or recalled relationships that were not passionate. And when they talked about passion, it wasn't just about sex. It was about depth of feeling. In my own life, the way I would describe it is that I still get butterflies in my stomach when I hear my wife's car pull into the driveway.

Some talked about relationships that were passionate at one point but something was lost along the way. And a good number of people talked about staying in relationships that were not passionate—certainly not fulfilling—for far too long. As people described their situations, it felt like the boiled frog syndrome I mentioned in Part II. For many of these people, the temperature was going up, but they didn't realize it until they were in the relationship far too long. Those who stuck it out for long periods of time describe many psychological scars—depression, anger, bitterness, remorse, sadness. Far too many described long periods of their lives that were devoid of excitement, creativity, and enjoyment. Quite a few felt they never recovered their "innocence." It was also clear that some never wanted to venture deep into a marriage or strong relationship again. How sad.

What's interesting to note is that outsiders often see the water is boiling. Sometimes friends provided the needed boost to help their frog-like friends from becoming dinner. Those without a strong network seemed to suffer more. They didn't have others they could fall back on for support or to offer objectivity. That is why one of the key recommendations is building a strong network of friends. Great friends and mentors can often support the introspection you need to make important decisions. In a busy life, people often don't make the time or avoid facing the potential disruptions that change may cause.

Earlier in this book, we introduced Carol, who was married to Victor. She had suffered the fear of disappointing others (husband, parents, children), stages of anger and resentment, and eventually depression. But with the counsel of a close friend, she realized that she needed to jump out of the boiling water. Once she saw an alternative, she realized even more so that her current situation was not working for her.

Victor was devastated when Carol asked for a divorce with an almost "nothing personal" air to it. He wanted to believe that something was wrong with her but was also afraid that perhaps he was flawed. As he began to take in data from friends, he sadly realized that he could not put "passion" back in the relationship—it simply was gone. After taking time to reflect, grieve, and extract the learnings, Victor found a woman whom he described to me as "someone I am truly passionate about—maybe for the first time now that I know what passion is." He thought he knew what love was but admitted later that he really didn't until experiencing it in a new situation. The real kicker was when he said, "The warning signs were all over, but I ignored them. If I had not been afraid to move on, I could have enjoyed a new, stronger relationship sooner."

The message from all these sages is the same: don't wait! If you are in a job or a relationship that doesn't satisfy you, move on, knowing that there are always costs to doing so. The question you have to answer is whether the potential benefits are far greater than the costs of remaining in an unfulfilling relationship.

LESSON 5: TAKE REASONABLE RISKS

Don Thomas was a remarkable astronaut who flew four missions into space in a matter of thirty-six months.[7] But the story of how Don got into orbit is one of taking reasonable career risks to reach his passion. When my wife first knew Don, he was an engineer working for Western Electric in a unit that she led. Don was passionate about becoming an astronaut, but he was not in a position that was fast-tracking him to NASA. He was not military, a pilot, or connected to NASA in any meaningful way. He asked my wife if she would support him in his quest and she said, "Of course," but asked him if he was willing to do what it might take to get in the right position to have that small shot at space.

His early attempts did not succeed. After endless paperwork, interviews with scores of references, and detailed background checks, he missed the final cuts. But he decided to quit a stable engineering job, move to Houston, and work for an organization much closer to NASA. There he might have a chance to demonstrate his abilities and build connections to NASA.

After making those sacrifices for several years, he finally made the cut into the NASA program and began training to be an astronaut. My wife and I had the wonderful opportunity to see him lift off at Cape Canaveral—a man who took the necessary risks to achieve his dream.

How many of us have a dream, but don't take the risks to achieve it? One government official we interviewed said, "Take appropriate risks in your life and career and do not be afraid of small failures."

Taking reasonable risks was one of the most frequent "looking back" recommendations from our panelists. Most learning occurs when you are trying new things, innovating, or exploring a new path. But risk is in the eyes of the beholder, and much research shows that people perceive risk differently. Or perhaps another way to put it is that each of us sees the risk of a situation differently. Some students love taking tests while others are nearly petrified of it. Some people race cars competitively while others are fearful of driving to the corner store.

Two factors go into risk. The first is your risk tolerance. Some people are more comfortable in situations of higher risk—a higher chance of failing. Others don't want to give that chance of failing even an inch of room and typically choose safe roads. The second factor is your perception of risk. Although I give many public speeches, I rarely feel that giving one is a high risk (although it may be). In contrast, I often meet someone at a speaking venue who says something like, "How do you do it? I would be petrified!" The difference is that these onlookers perceive a high risk of failure, but today I do not. When I started my career, I was thrown into several speaking assignments sweating and gasping for breath, and I learned some painful lessons. The point is, I learned.

That is the lesson from our interviewees who told us to "take more risks early in life." Many felt that their moments of risk were some of the best learning experiences in their lives. In fact, most of the people I spoke with actually recalled those moments fondly. For example, Arnie, who made a major job shift at Abbott, said, "While it was painful at the time, I actually started to feel good about it, and it gave me new skills I didn't have. Now I feel like a pro. It is something that differentiated me on the way up."

Some early psychological studies by David McClelland focused on achievement motivation in children by using a game. The game consisted of tossing a ring onto a pole, but the children were not given any direction as to what exact distance to stand from the pole. He found that kids with a high achievement motive did calculated guesses and were good at selecting a distance at which they were the farthest away but could still get the ring into the pole. Also, McClelland found this trait of calculated risks to be very prominent in successful entrepreneurs.[8]

Casinos also understand this in a big way—their income depends on it. Stingy slot machines begin to sit idle. There is a fine balance between the players getting enough positive reinforcement and taking a risk of losing that is stimulating. That's the message here.

Last, our panelists told us, "Don't bet the farm on one decision; take risks that will stretch you, create new learnings, and increase your feelings of accomplishment." They also cautioned against second-guessing yourself continuously. You will make mistakes— that is what will stretch you—but you should allow yourself the freedom to reverse a decision that is not working out. If you think you want to major in engineering and you are not stimulated in that field, change. If you have dated someone for three years and it is moving in the wrong direction, change. If you have committed to a life path that is not bringing fulfillment, change.

One of the lotto ads in my area used to say, "You have to be in it to win it!" The same is true in life. In the next chapter, I look at five other important arts to becoming fulfilled.

13

Life Lessons

Part II

> *It is good to have an end to journey towards; but
> it is the journey that matters, in the end.*
>
> —Ursula K. Le Guin

In the previous chapter, I shared five practical strategies from the wisdom of those who were the most fulfilled. In this chapter, we continue our journey to understanding the art of becoming and staying fulfilled.

LESSON 6: NEVER STOP LEARNING—NEVER!

Not only does your body need nourishment and strengthening, but so does your mind. Most of our interviewees described the importance of continuous learning in a variety of ways.

For example, the TV quiz show *Jeopardy!* pitted IBM's supercomputer Watson against the best performers the show had seen in recent years. While there was a lot of hoopla leading up to the event, after two episodes, it was clear that humans could no longer compete with the computer when it came to memory. Watson won the competition hands down.

Technology has continued to replace labor. Some of that we like—pushing a button and having toast or pastries within seconds instead of taking the time to cook something over the stove—but when it costs us our jobs, we like it less. An increasing number of people are facing job obsolescence. According to author Douglas Rushkoff, "We are living in an economy where productivity is no longer the goal, employment is."[1] Auto workers, accountants, or radiologists in Western countries have been replaced by cheaper resources in India; butchers have been replaced by packaged meat suppliers; printers like my uncle have been replaced by digital printing—Daniel Pink tells us that if something can be automated, it will replace a job, sooner or later.[2]

Why is this happening so much today? Automation is primarily due to the rate of change: higher expectations of customers for new and better products, easy access to global markets, and speed of technological change—check out your latest phone. Apple's customers expect at least one major new phone release annually. If you think this is just related to the last recession, forget about it. This is a permanent change. It took centuries for agriculture to change, hundreds of years for transportation to change, but since the Industrial Revolution, such change has occurred in decades. Since the Internet revolution intermarried with computer technology and global access, change is happening in years, months, or minutes.

New businesses, products, and processes are being created in fractions of the time it took historically, creating obsolescence for some and opportunity for others. When the gold rush hit Alaska in the 1800s, some people made fortunes while others lost all they had. For the most part, the biggest winners were not the miners and gold panners but the businesses that sold the shovels, picks, food, and entertainment to them. Saloons and brothels grew rich while most miners came home empty-handed. For every change and innovation, something else will be displaced. The key is to ensure that it is not you.

So how do you do that? Our grandparents could bank on developing a skill or expertise that would last them a lifetime. One generation later, my father, uncle, and some of their cousins saw jobs they had relied on—in printing, meat cutting, steel, or accounting—disappear. Many baby boomers have not been able to count on one career path based on skills that were learned in high school or college. While undoubtedly dating myself in the eyes of many readers, I remember how much time was spent in my own school years learning slide rules or mechanical drawing. Can you imagine how useless those skills are today?

With the last two recessions, many people were cut down before they could reach the magic retirement or pension age. Many were scrambling for low-paying jobs that did not use their skills just to ensure some income. This is not what they planned but what they have had to do because of change. For younger baby boomers and Gen Xers, it has been tougher because many did not get close to retirement; for many of them, there were dramatic changes taking place while they were in their late thirties or forties.

Specialist or Generalist?

While elders were whispering the word *plastics* to Dustin Hoffman in the movie *The Graduate*, that advice represented an increasing trend of specialization. "Become a specialist" was the motto for many years. "Don't become an auto mechanic, become a tire specialist, an audio specialist, a transmission specialist. Don't become a general practice doctor—become a cardiologist or brain surgeon," was the current wisdom. Well, this has led to a dilemma today. We have people, often with dated skills, who are a mile deep in their expertise but only an inch deep in anything else. That worked pretty well when we didn't have to think about changing jobs or professions.

Today, millennials can't even think this way. They must assume that they could have three, four, five, or more "careers." This means learning some short-term, specific skills that will help you in the short run but developing other long-term skills that will be valuable as you change jobs or cross career lines in the future. For example, when I began doing tax auditing as a part-time job, computers were not able to help much; they often made more errors than they fixed. Not long after, the long tables of students with calculators and a strong knowledge of tax code were replaced by students with more rudimentary knowledge of tax code because they were simply verifying that the computer did what it was supposed to do; they performed simple logic checks. Most of those employed at that time had no idea that their work would soon be shipped to India to be performed equally well (or better) at lower labor costs. One of my tax bench buddies used to say, "I wish I didn't have to do this boring work, but it pays the bills." Not anymore; he got his wish!

The trend today is to compile a suite of skills that are often held by excellent generalists. In human resources, for example, staying strictly within benefits or compensation may be fulfilling if that is where your passion is, and future technology and business needs allow you to stay there in the future. But if your passion is to achieve more senior levels, a portfolio of skills and experiences across a host of HR areas—training, leader development, coaching, change management, succession planning, talent acquisition—and overall business acumen will lead to a more rounded set of credentials that may help you earn one of the top spots.

Carl is a key executive within a federal agency. But only ten years ago, he was still aspiring to a managerial role. He was selected for his top job because of his wide range of experiences over the past decade. He took steps that included being an individual contributor in strategic planning, a manager in HR, a top leader in IT, and a controller in finance. These broad experiences enabled him to be considered for a top multidisciplinary role. Individuals with experience in only one function had only a fraction of the understanding of the organization that he had. Whom would you promote?

Life Skills

The key today is developing some marketable skills that can be used now while honing important life skills that will be valuable over time. For example, communication skills were singled out by many of our wise panelists. Most felt that their communication skills are important throughout life, whether it is presenting oneself for a job, a promotion, or an idea.

Many we interviewed spoke about the importance of effective writing skills and even astute body language. In the book *The Presentation Secrets of Steve Jobs*, author Carmine Gallo attributes much of Jobs's success to his ability to do all of the above.[3] His presentations were knockouts that convinced the world to do different things, and his body language exuded confidence and passion.

No matter what job you take, group you join, or spouse you marry, communication is probably one of the biggest secrets to success. Start early, speak publicly, take courses to hone those skills, and be careful of over- or inappropriate use of e-mail or texts. And don't forget great listening skills.

Listening is rated as one of the worst skills of most people—most of us want to tell, not listen. However, Tina Sung, vice president of government transformation and agency partnerships at the Partnership for Public Service in Washington, DC, has a different view of her success. She said, "Deep listening is one of the most important skills you can develop."

After coming back from a meeting together, I asked her what she heard at the meeting. I was amazed at what she walked away with. Most of her understanding was never stated explicitly in the meeting; it was what she read between the lines that counted. Having worked with this organization for some time, I was surprised at how accurate she was. Listening is particularly important in relationships. Nobody wants to be around someone who does all the talking; after a while, it is just boring. Take time to hone your listening skills.

Other skills that tend to carry over careers, and relationships, include good decision-making skills, the ability to empathize with others, the ability to relax and turn off, and the ability to be a good team player. Almost everything we do throughout our lives involves teams of one sort or another.

Continuous Learning

Part of the challenge today—in contrast to that of earlier generations—is not counting on certain skills learned early in life to carry you through retirement. Today, almost any job or career will have rapidly evolving demands. Take computer programmers, for example. When I was in college, the computer programming languages Algol, Fortran, and Cobol were all sure tickets to a good job—talk about dating myself! But if I was counting on mastery of those codes of yesteryear for my income today, I would be broke. New, more powerful programming languages like C++ and Visual Basic replaced those, and languages continue to be replaced at even faster rates. You can't stand still. If you want to remain a viable programmer, you will constantly be forced to upgrade your skills and learn new coding languages.

And this is not only for technology skills but for traditional workers as well. Factory workers are expected to be smart workers, managing the operation of intelligent machines and automated tools such as lathes and welders through computers rather than being the primary source of skill and intelligence operating such machinery.

Organizations want knowledge workers—those who can leverage evolving technology—more and more. In the building trades, plumbers, carpenters, and electricians must have a better understanding of new materials and complex, integrated control systems that continue to evolve every year. This requires additional skills—the traditional body of knowledge within a given trade and knowledge of technology. For example, auto mechanics repairing cars today must use computer analyzers to interface with onboard computers to diagnose problems with everything from emissions to fuel flow to transmission operation. And when something is broken, they are more likely to replace an electronic sensor or computer module than to repair such components.

Noncareer Learning

What about noncareer-related learning? Let's say I want to hang out with cool friends or connect with my nephews and nieces. It's not going to happen sitting at my desk with my old phone or writing a letter. It's not going to happen with e-mail; they don't use it (except maybe to tame their parent!). Today, it's going to be texting; it's going to be on social media sites.

A recent intern told me that Facebook was "so yesterday," as her friends have moved on to Instagram and other sites (which may sound old by the time you read this). Try asking your kids or nieces and nephews about Palm Pilots or Lotus Notes. Or do what I did— bring a deck of Hollerith cards to your office and ask someone how to store the data. Most of the folks will simply go silent, wondering if you arrived by stagecoach.

The same is true in strong relationships with spouses, close family, or friends. While they may overlook some of your technological ineptness, they will not overlook your inability to grow and develop as a person. Nobody wants to show up at a party today with the Beav (quiz for those under fifty), the Fonz (quiz for those under forty), or Newhart (quiz for those under thirty). People would wonder what rock you have been living under. But it's not just dress, manner, or language (yes, important) but whether you are evolving with the other person. Are you growing into new things together or growing apart? Has one of you evolved an interest in the arts or crafts while the other is still the exact same person from twenty years ago?

While this is not an easy conversation to have among intimate friends or partners, ignoring it doesn't mean it is not happening. Charlotte, a therapist I knew years ago, told me, "One day I just woke up and realized that my husband hadn't changed in twenty years, and this is one reason I am not feeling very fulfilled in my life." In her professional life, she was growing and learning. But in her personal life, she was stagnating. Her husband was the same comfy being he was when he was twenty-five. She was forty-five and wanted more from life. He wasn't interested in changing after much conversation over four years. She filed for divorce.

Her husband couldn't figure it out. He had never stopped to think about whether he and she were evolving together. Were they still aligned with their future direction? Were they each engaged with their lifestyle? Was each of them growing their capabilities—listening skills, appreciation of art or football, golf handicap, child rearing—in complementary ways? Quite often, relationships end when one person has evolved and the other has not, or when they are evolving in different directions—a clear case of misalignment.

Keep on learning, which also implies making changes, when the familiar and comfortable is no longer working. The definition of insanity has been posited as continuing to do the same thing that hasn't worked before and hoping for a different outcome.

LESSON 7: STICK TO YOUR VALUES AND SPIRITUALITY

The idea of spirituality and values is another key element of the art of staying fulfilled, underscored by so many of my interviewees. While many of them were not religious in a strict sense, most talked about having clear values, the importance of raising children with good values, and the ability to stay aligned with your values.

Some stressed spirituality—having a deep inner sense of peace or tranquility—that was tied to their religious or other beliefs. Some noted that you don't have to be religious to be spiritual. Some practiced yoga or other forms of meditation. Some were Buddhists and many were mainstream Christians, Muslims, or Jews. Regardless of specific beliefs, those beliefs seemed most valuable when they were able to use them for guidance or for reflection.

Religious writings like the Bible and the Koran provide clarity to many on what is right and wrong. Some of these values have been baked in at very early ages, providing clear guideposts for actions and behaviors. Said one interviewee, "While I have told lies occasionally during my life, I feel guilty or badly about them," clearly limiting those transgressions.

One pharmaceutical executive talked about discovering yoga and meditation when he was in his early forties. He said, "It changed my life. I have not gone a week since then without meditating, often every morning." He is now in his early sixties.

In the work setting, we have seen many instances of the role and importance of values. When values such as ethical principles are violated—think the Enron debacle or the subprime mortgage banking scandals—the public is outraged. Some companies, such as WD-40 or Johnson & Johnson, have established values or credos to provide guidance to their employees. Earlier in this book, we mentioned the views of Garry Ridge, the CEO of WD-40 Company. He posited, "If you have good values, you don't have to prescribe hundreds of rules and policies. You simply need to ask someone, did you behave according to the values?"

Johnson & Johnson has had a famous credo that provides guidance on how members of the company should treat customers, employees, suppliers, and their shareholders for more than seventy years now. It has helped them stay the course and, when they have had crises, enabled them to examine their behaviors against the Johnson & Johnson credo to ensure that they are doing the right thing.

Jim Leighton, former COO of Boulder Brands, told us, "Aligned values are the guard rails of fulfilled individuals, teams, organizations, and even nations. When those guard rails come down or are broken, and they will, they must be replaced or repaired immediately, no questions asked."

One clear way in which values help us become fulfilled is in helping us choose behaviors that are consistent with what we believe is important—integrity, trust, respect, openness, collaboration, or any number of other important values. By having a clear sense of what your values are, and what they are not, it allows you to become personally aligned—whether with your partner in life, your employer, or both. Human beings want consistency. We like it when someone says he or she believes in being transparent and consistently shares information openly.

The other use of values described by our interviewees is in figuring out what has gone wrong. Why am I stuck or unhappy? Often, misalignment is the culprit. If you have friends who think it is okay to steal and you don't, it is going to create enormous tension because you have to decide whether to live your values or go along with the crowd in doing something you are uncomfortable with—it is a tug-of-war between your social needs and who you stand for.

Some of our panelists describe marriages gone badly, often due to different values. One friend described her husband as never having grown up. When I pressed her, she said he still loved to smoke pot, spend nights with his band, and just goof off. She said those were not her values—she wanted respectability, which in her mind went with a more responsible job, spending social evenings with people who were into the arts, and avoiding drugs. Eventually, they parted ways.

Others described leaving jobs or companies when they felt their values were compromised. For example, one vice president of a health care company described how uncomfortable he became as executives in his company were beginning to cross an ethical line. He worried that some health care product tests were being covered up and that the whole truth was not being shared with the FDA or other authorities. He began worrying about patients. Having come from a company in which such honesty was paramount, he felt that he needed to get out. He didn't want to be part of something that might injure or harm others.

Think about your values. As I asked you earlier in this book, what are the most important values to you? How well do you think you are aligned with those values in your day-to-day behaviors? Do you live your values in all that you do? Can you remember times in your life when those values were in conflict or when you were in a situation that violated them? How did you feel? How did you respond? These types of questions can help you stay aligned with who you are or want to be. Values go hand in hand with life goals. They are the "how" we wish to live as we head toward our life goals. Know your values and nurture them.

Lesson 8: Resilience—Find the Silver Lining

Most people get knocked down many times during their lives; the winners get up and try again. Many of our interviewees talked about the importance of developing resilience to setbacks, personal failures, or medical adversity.

Grit is a recent term defined by Angela Duckworth in her TED talk as "passion and perseverance for very long-term goals." According to Duckworth, grit is a predictor of success. Grit is about living life focusing on the end goal without losing motivation despite setbacks.[4]

Take Mike Schultz, a competitive snowmobiler who lost his leg in a crash in 2008.[5] Upon passing another competitor, he lost control of the vehicle and was thrown from the machine. He hit the ground so hard that he was looking at the bottom of his foot in front of his eyes. Sadly, the leg could not be saved. For most people, this would mean retirement and perhaps time to have a desk job. But "Monster" Schultz was fitted with a prosthetic leg and got back on the snowmobile. This is true grit, but his story doesn't end here. The best leg that doctors could fit him with couldn't take the impact of snowmobiling. So what did this true competitor do? He designed his own leg! He took parts from mountain bikes and built a prosthesis that allowed him not only to compete but to win silver at the Moto X Racing Adaptive only seven months after losing his leg. The following year, when the X Games added adaptive snocross, he took gold. For most people, this would have been enough. But Mike wanted to do more for others facing similar situations. He started a business using his new designs to supply these tougher-than-real-legs prostheses for former army amputees and others who wanted to get up and compete.

Now compare Mike's story to most of our lives. Most of our fulfilled interviewees had setbacks, often ones that people who knew them didn't realize. But they had a turning point when they mentally started to compete again and turned bad luck or situations into gold.

Take a look back at a handful of situations in your life that have been disappointments—lost jobs, spouses, accidents, medical setbacks—and how you reacted in the situation. Were you like "Monster" Schultz? While you can't go back and change those earlier situations, thinking about what you might have done differently to get the ball rolling again should help you when the next setback occurs.

Resilience is an area that can be helped greatly by a support network—friends, family, spouse. Many of our fulfilled panelists describe how important one or two other people were to them during moments of doubt or during setbacks. Often a mentor or coach encouraged them to stand up and fight, to stop and rethink their direction, or to let go of a toxic relationship. Most of our advisors said that the hardest thing to do is to remove the emotion and look at the facts. Quite often the facts are not as dismal as the perceived setback, and even when they are, they provide a baseline for the climb out of the downward spiral.

Many scuba accidents could have been avoided by quick, clear thinking—sadly, many deaths have resulted from panic and giving up. If you are out of air at twenty feet, you may well think about quickly moving to the surface, but if you do that at seventy feet, you may well kill yourself. At seventy feet, you want to quickly move to your diving buddy and share air with him or her. That split-second thinking about the facts can be the difference between life and death.

A key lesson in all these stories is perseverance. Even when things are dismal, some individuals are able to rally and overcome some of their maladies. Many people we have interviewed have talked about mental toughness, saying that resilience and the ability to maintain a positive mental attitude was crucial to their eventual success.

Lesson 9: Give and Get

One area that we did not anticipate hearing about as frequently as we did is giving back, or just giving. A particularly strong voice came from the more seasoned interviewees. Interestingly, we found evidence of this in our millennial study as well—a desire to contribute in a bigger way to society, our planet, and others.

I have served on a number of volunteer boards over the years, and I am continually reminded of this desire to contribute when I see the passion of volunteers. One board that I serve on has people who have been highly successful in their own right and do not need to serve to build up their résumés or egos. They come from big companies such as Microsoft, small entrepreneurial ventures, government, NGOs, associations, or universities.

Interestingly, while some have retired from long careers in one occupation, they are highly active today in volunteer work or giving back. When I chat with these folks, they all say that despite the incredible time it takes to serve on the board, they feel fulfilled by what the organization or association is doing. They feel that they are helping the organization reach its full potential and that they are helping the profession and younger people who have just started their careers.

In the work that I do with organizations to increase their employee engagement, we often find that those who are most engaged are also the ones who volunteer for additional tasks inside and outside of their organizations. This is a virtuous circle of fulfillment feeding fulfillment. Consider how you give back. Are you part of volunteer groups that could bring happiness to you and others? Are you coaching a football team or tutoring aspiring students? Are you giving time to your community to perhaps help clean up the streets or environment? Out of the people we interviewed, I have observed the greatest fulfillment in those who are leveraging the potential of others, whether that is helping people physically or mentally or helping them on the road to success and fulfillment.

There is a group in New York City called Rosie's Theatre Kids. Many are inner-city kids who the agency told me had been spending their time in gang activities, drugs, or nonproductive activities. Fortunately, dedicated volunteers are helping these individuals find purpose and enjoyment, increasing their sense of worth. The volunteers have brought kids of all ages from street corners, crack houses, broken homes, and homeless shelters into a musical community that would blow your mind. These kids have learned to sing, dance, and entertain in a way that brought tears to my eyes. All I had to do was watch the faces, the smiles, the sense of accomplishment, and the recognition that they have something to offer the world.

After I heard the backstory of these kids, I wondered how it was possible. And yet a few volunteers have changed the lives—the future trajectory—of hundreds. It was impossible to leave the performance unmoved. Without these volunteers, and the thousands around the globe that do give back to groups just like this, hope would not be possible.

They remind me very much of the story of the starfish. The story goes something like this: A girl is frantically running up and down a beach tossing as many tide-stranded starfish as she can back into the ocean, granting them another day of life. A man standing nearby, looking at the thousands of starfish that she can't possibly save, tells her that she can never save all the starfish. He asks her why she bothers. She tosses in another one and says, "I made a difference to that one." Who will you make a difference to today?

LESSON 10: CHECK IN WITH YOURSELF REGULARLY—FORCE IT!

If you were running a company, would you check your progress every ten years? If you were a marathon runner, would you check your progress once a year? If you were an avid football fan, would you wait to see the final standings of your favorite team at the end of the season? Of course not, and you should not do that with your life.

This lesson is tricky because we tend to lose vigilance when things are going well. One night my wife and I were driving home and I had had such a good time that I wanted to revel in the moment, but I forgot to check my gasoline, and we ran out. Part of the reason we have gauges in our cars, and in our lives, is to help us get feedback that enables us to make decisions about the future.

We're going along in a job or a relationship and everything seems to be positive. But gradually, things may be changing. One of my relatives was in a relationship that seemed to be going well, but there were telltale signs that it was changing—and not positively. He and his significant other were not the best communicators. They didn't take time to stop and discuss their relationship. Negative assumptions crept in, and the next thing he knew, she was moving out.

One of our interviewees was a middle-aged man who talked about being encouraged by his parents to pursue medical school. He had loved his early schooling, had a great memory for things like anatomy, and enjoyed his time with classmates. But as he got into medical school, things began to change. He didn't like the pressure and was not a big fan of the operational side of things; but eventually he finished. He struggled with his internship, feeling that things must get better. He chafed at his early medical practice that was connected to a local hospital because he was constantly stressed and went home most nights with headaches, feeling depressed. He began to drink heavily.

The sad fact is that he didn't stop to take his temperature. Why was he more and more disenchanted with his career path? Was he doing it to follow through on commitments to his parents? Was he doing it because his spouse loved being married to a doctor? Was he doing it for the money or prestige? After fifteen years, he took serious stock of his situation and realized that he could have saved twelve years of unfulfilled time because he didn't seriously assess himself along the way. This story has a more tragic ending than most; he ended up committing suicide. He could not bear the incredible unhappiness and loss of his potential. While this may feel like an exceptional case, it is not. About forty thousand people in the United States kill themselves every year, many because they lose hope.[6]

Sunk Cost

The previous story illustrates one of the great "ahas" of those who have been around the block. Often, we fail to bail out of something because we have made increasing commitments that have psychologically "locked" us in. The doctor in the story had made an investment in college, then a medical program, then an internship, then starting a practice, and so forth.

These commitments are highly public—parents who are watching you succeed in medical or law school, friends who have watched you date and marry someone, a mentor who has encouraged you to specialize in something, and so forth. The more public a commitment is, and the more you put your ego on the line, the harder it is to acknowledge to both yourself and others that it was a mistake.

As I mentioned earlier in this book, it was not easy telling my friends in college that playing cards was not my life priority or telling members of my band that I had to limit my practice time to ensure that I would graduate with the grades I needed to succeed. And if you are like me, you may wait much longer than you should before you look yourself in the mirror and then take the hard step of announcing your intentions to others.

Take Stock at Least Annually

We found some of our fulfilled panel taking stock of their life as often as quarterly. But an annual review may be sufficient for many people. Or, as you pass through different stages of your life path, it is worthwhile to take stock. If you are finishing high school, you face multiple choices. When you finish one job or a degree, it is a good time to assess where you are as you head toward your life goals.

In Part III of this book, which explored the science of fulfillment, I provided a number of tools for visualizing and measuring your life progress. Use them or adapt them to work for you. One important caution: be honest with yourself in the assessments. If you don't, you are only fooling yourself. One thing that I find very helpful is to use a sheet of paper or a spreadsheet and create two columns. On the left, I like to list what is helping me become fulfilled on my life path and, on the right, what is not fulfilling me at this time. It is a simple but powerful way to get a quick feel for where I am.

The second thing I do is create another list of all the things I spend time on (within reason) on a different sheet of paper or spreadsheet. Then I mark whether I wish I were spending more or less time in this activity—a measure of enjoyment or fulfillment at the moment. Last, I create a column in which I simply check whether each activity is related to the drivers of my life goals or not. Not everything you do every day is directly tied to the drivers of your life goals. We must do things that are asked or required of us by others (perhaps babysitting for a friend), by organizations we work with, or by government (waiting in line to get your driver's license renewed). Two things you can quickly observe are these:

- What is the percentage of your time that is devoted to drivers of your life goals? You can get highly quantitative in doing this (counting up how your time is spent) or calculate it a bit more subjectively. If your time is mostly spent on activities that are not leading to fulfillment, it is time to take stock and think about changes you can make. I almost always tweak my balance of time and activities based on this feedback—sometimes a small amount and other times a great deal.

- How has your balance changed over time? This of course requires keeping your assessments from earlier times. I have found this absolutely fascinating because activities, commitments, and direction keep changing throughout our lives. Some of the changes we might expect based on our plans, but other things creep in over time that squeeze out important long-range priorities that will bring you fulfillment. When I began this book, I stated that each of us has approximately 34 million minutes to shape our lives and our fulfillment. If we are controlling our own fulfillment, we need to ensure that the gusto is not squeezed out by activity creep—activities that begin eating up more and more time but are not adding to our overall value as a person. In the last year, you have spent approximately 525,000 minutes of your lifetime. Was it spent in a way that is helping you become more fulfilled?

Take stock of yourself regularly. You are your own pilot through life and you need good feedback about how well your journey is going.

Epilogue

Putting It All Together

Before we close, I want to return to the story I opened with because it brings together much of what we have shared throughout this book. If you remember Marisa, who overcame stage-four pancreatic cancer, you will recall that I had been working with her firm to help transform its culture. At that time, we were using a strategic scorecarding process to help their business become aligned with its goals. The strategic scorecarding process helped leaders translate their vision and strategy for the organization into measures that captured the most important aspects that they needed to manage—key people, customers, suppliers, community, shareholders, and operations.

But it didn't stop there. The formula for successful change was getting the rest of the organization to understand those measures (Why are we measuring this? What is the strategy?) so they could best support the strategy and direction. That process helped create huge change in their organization and great financial results by reducing client losses, increasing employee engagement, reducing service times, and adjusting a variety of other key success factors.

When I sat down with Marisa recently, she described how she took those same principles and applied them to her life—at first physical survival and later to all aspects of her life. When I began this book, I said there is no such thing as a perfect ability to predict success or fulfillment, but you can stack the odds in your favor.

That is exactly what Marisa did. She focused on her life goal and did everything in her power to manage her life drivers. She is a role model for me—and now for many others—of how we must draw on all of our energy to achieve our dreams.

ENJOY BEFORE YOU DIE

A final observation from our panel of fulfilled individuals: don't defer until death—enjoy the ride! Take Justin, who complained that he had waited too long to begin enjoying life. He had parents who focused on his education and his musical interests early on, followed by rigorous high school tutors and acceptance into a premier university. Of course, it was assumed that an undergraduate degree would not be enough for him. They wanted him to complete his education, which meant getting a law or medical degree, getting married, and having grandchildren for his parents. His parents had a wonderful plan—for them!

Unfortunately, this was not what fulfilled Justin. He didn't want to practice law. Instead, he wanted to teach high school students, enjoy some sports, enjoy movies, and hang out with friends once in a while. But there was never enough time for that. Unfortunately, he was only mediocre in law because he did not have the passion to master it, spent a huge amount of time at the office trying to keep up with peers who did, had a number of failed relationships, and missed much of his prime athletic years. His mastery of various musical instruments was neither successful nor very fulfilling.

Before he knew it, he was in his forties and living with regret. The advice from both those who were highly fulfilled early in life and those who were not is to balance the long and short term. Too much focus on the here and now—enjoying friends, partying, watching videos, or hobbies—is likely to hurt your chances of reaching your life goals. However, the reverse is also the case. As the saying goes, "All work and no play make Jack a dull boy." Constantly deferring gratification until late in life often led to regrets and disenchantment among those with whom we talked. The trick appears to be balancing the two.

The most successful and fulfilled told us that they had a plan and stuck with it, but they also found time to relax and enjoy some of the fleeting fulfillments along the way—hiking in the mountains, gardening, travel, reading nonwork-related books, spending time with friends, or playing sports. They also seemed particularly adept at adjusting their nonwork activities at different stages of life. Many participated in strenuous sports at earlier ages such as football but adapted later to racquetball and maybe later again to golf. Others talked about mountain climbing or paragliding, but as they aged, they still remained active hikers or swimmers. Still others added reflective hobbies later on—yoga, reading, or long walks.

As a colleague said to me in my thirties, "Bill, take time to smell the roses." He was right. I will always remember his advice and still do today. Whether during a run, a walk, or even bicycling, I will stop when I see a patch of roses and take in the scent and beauty, and it reminds me that I need to continuously balance different aspects of my life. I deserve it and so do you.

Send Us Your Own Story

We would love to hear from readers with their own stories of goal-setting, overcoming obstacles, personal achievement, and the road to fulfillment that they are following—or have followed—in their own life. Please contact the author at http://www.wschiemann .com/fulfilled.

About the Author

William A. Schiemann, PhD, GPHR

Bill Schiemann is the CEO of Metrus Group. He is a thought leader in human resources, employee engagement, and fulfillment, having authored scores of articles and multiple books on talent management, including *The Rise of HR*, coedited with Dave Ulrich and Libby Sartain (sponsored by HRCI, 2015); *Hidden Drivers of Success: Leveraging Employee Insights for Strategic Advantage* (SHRM, 2013); *The ACE Advantage: How Smart Companies Unleash Talent for Optimal Performance* (SHRM, 2012); *Reinventing Talent Management: How to Maximize Performance in the New Marketplace* (published by Wiley and SHRM, 2009); and *Bullseye! Hitting Your Strategic Targets through High-Impact Measurement* (The Free Press, 1999).

Dr. Schiemann is a frequent global keynote speaker and workshop facilitator for many public and private forums around the globe. He is a fellow and scholar of the Society for Industrial and Organizational Psychology (SIOP). He received a PhD in organizational psychology from the University of Illinois. Follow him on Twitter at @Wschiemann and on LinkedIn at William Schiemann.

Acknowledgments

It goes without saying that a book of this type does not happen without the dedication and support of many people.

First and foremost, a *sincere* round of thanks goes to the scores of folks who so openly shared their inner thoughts and feelings about work, family, and life. Their stories, and insights, are the heart of this book and give the structure life. In addition, I owe so much to friends and family who provided many rounds of feedback to my ideas, draft versions, and the design of the book cover. Special thanks go to Jim Steele, Laura Mindek, Matthew Mangino, Rita Pettiford, Brian Morgan, Ian Ziskin, Susan Bershad, Carl Persing, Steve Ginsburgh, Amy Mysel, Christine Hutchinson, Alex Garcia, Leslie Guth, and as always, my wife and Metrus colleague, Valeria Schiemann, who all provided important evaluations at various stages of the research and manuscript. I am indebted to all of them for their insights and help in overcoming some of my blind spots. As I write these words, I am sure that I am forgetting one or more key people who should also be on this list, and I apologize for that oversight. So many people were a part of this six-plus-year effort, and I am grateful to them all.

I would like to acknowledge the Metrus team, all of whom have been supportive throughout the process. This research and writing effort required far more perseverance than other major projects and

I appreciate the support, help, and encouragement of my colleagues during the many months—years—in bringing this to fruition.

Finally, great thanks to Ron Sauder, my publisher, who has been both a friend and colleague for many years. We finally have had a chance to collaborate on this book. He has helped me think through how to reach the people that would most benefit from this work and has been a great editor and *conscience* to me as we have moved through this effort. My interns Danielle Novotny and Kyle Dobson have been an incredible help during the finishing stages of this book, providing research input, countless corrections, and insight into the millennial world. Jennifer Bruce and Katerin Lopera, my prior two interns, were instrumental in earlier work on the book, ranging from research to the development of a prototype app. Of course, my valued executive assistant and marketing partner Colette Tarsan has provided her usual insights and support.

Like Newton, I too feel that I stand on the shoulders of giants before me, such as Martin Seligman, Deepak Chopra, Ed Diener, Sonja Lyubomirsky, David and Wendy Ulrich, Marshall Goldsmith, Aaron Hurst, David Campbell, Marisa Harris, and many others— too many to list—who in their own ways have broken ground and stimulated thinking in this emerging field.

W. Schiemann, June 2016

Notes

INTRODUCTION

1 Ed Diener, "Defining and Measuring Happiness (or Subjective Well-Being)," *Discoveries at the Diener's Lab*, 2013, http://internal.psychology.illinois.edu/~ediener/discoveries.html.

2 S. Lyubomirsky, *The How of Happiness: A New Approach to Getting the Life You Want* (New York: Penguin Books, 2008).

3 M. E. Seligman, *Authentic Happiness: Using the New Positive Psychology to Realize Your Potential for Lasting Fulfillment* (New York: Free Press, 2002).

4 Caroline A. Miller and Michael B. Frisch, *Creating Your Best Life: The Ultimate Life List Guide* (New York: Sterling, 2009).

5 For more information, see the "Authentic Happiness" website, available at https://www.authentichappiness.sas.upenn.edu.

6 Dan Diamond, "Just 8% of People Achieve Their New Year's Resolutions: Here's How They Do It," *Forbes*, January 1, 2013, accessed June 10, 2015, http://www.forbes.com/sites/dandiamond/2013/01/01/just-8-of-people-achieve-their-new-years-resolutions-heres-how-they-did-it.

CHAPTER 2

1 Pete Wells, "The Burger Remains a Work in Progress: Shake Shack Struggles with Inconsistency," *New York Times*, February 21,

2012, http://www.nytimes.com/2012/02/22/dining/reviews/
shake-shack-struggles-with-inconsistency.html?ref=danny
meyer&_r=0.

CHAPTER 4

1 Thomas L. Friedman, *The World Is Flat: A Brief History of the Twenty-First Century* (New York: Farrar, Straus and Giroux, 2005).
2 D. H. Pink, *To Sell Is Human: The Surprising Truth about Moving Others* (New York: Riverhead Books, 2012).

CHAPTER 5

1 Kris Garcia, "Why Choose DonorsChoose.org?," http://www .donorschoose.org/careers.
2 Amy Adkins, "Majority of U.S. Employees Not Engaged despite Gains In 2014," *Gallup*, January 28, 2015, http://www .gallup.com/poll/181289/majority-employees-not-engaged -despite-gains-2014.aspx.
3 Aon Hewitt, "2015 Trends in Global Employee Engagement: Making Engagement Happen," http://www.aon.com/ attachments/human-capital-consulting/2015-Trends-in -Global-Employee-Engagement-Report.pdf.

CHAPTER 6

1 "Carl Lewis Biography," *Biography.com*, http://www.biography .com/people/carl-lewis-40103.
2 "Missy Franklin Biography," *Biography.com*, http://www .biography.com/people/missy-franklin-20903291.
3 Karen Crouse, "Second Wind for Michael Phelps, as a Swimmer and a Person," *New York Times*, April 17, 2015, accessed May 6, 2015, http://www.nytimes.com/2015/04/19/sports/

olympics/michael-phelps-the-person-is-back-not-just-the
-swimmer.html?_r=0.

4 Brian Alexander, "After the Gold: Olympic Medalists Struggle with Real Life," *NBC News*, February 22, 2014, accessed April 15, 2015, http://www.nbcnews.com/storyline/sochi
-olympics/after-gold-olympic-medalists-struggle-real-life
-n35561.

5 Malcolm Moore, "Top Chinese Gymnast Found Begging on the Street," *Telegraph*, July 18, 2011, accessed June 2, 2015, http://www.telegraph.co.uk/news/worldnews/asia/china/
8645237/Top-Chinese-gymnast-found-begging-on-the
-street.html.

6 "Matthew 22:36–40," *Bible Gateway*, accessed April 15, 2015, https://www.biblegateway.com/passage/?search=Matthew+22:
36-40#en-NIV-23912.

7 "Mahatma Gandhi Biography," *Biography.com*, http://www
.biographyonline.net/politicians/indian/gandhi.html.

8 "Martin Luther King Biography," *Biography.com*, http://www
.biographyonline.net/politicians/american/martin-luther-king
.html.

9 "Triologue," *Stratford Festival*, accessed April 15, 2015, http://
www.stratfordfestival.ca/uploadedFiles/Stratford/Education
_and_Training/Teachers/PDF_and_Doc_Files/Triologue.pdf
?n=1761.

10 Steward D. Friedman, "Work + Home + Community + Self," *Harvard Business Review*, September 2014, accessed December 4, 2014, https://hbr.org/2014/09/work-home-community-self.

11 "Andre Agassi on Hating Tennis," *NBC News*, March 12, 2014; Matt Lauer, "'Open': Andre Agassi Talks Life on and Off the Court," *NBC News*, 2010, accessed May 6, 2015, http://www.nbcnews.com/id/21134540/vp/38950758
#38950758.

12 William H. Whyte, *The Organization Man* (Garden City, NY: Doubleday, 1956).

CHAPTER 7

1 "Condoleezza Rice Details Her Civil Rights Roots," *NPR Books*, October 13, 2010, accessed May 24, 2016, http://www.npr.org/templates/story/story.php?storyId=130425923; Anthony Tommasini, "Condoleezza Rice on Piano," *New York Times*, April 9, 2006, http://www.nytimes.com/2006/04/09/arts/music/09tomm.html?pagewanted=3; Marcus Mabry, *Twice as Good: Condoleezza Rice and Her Path to Power* (New York: Modern Times, 2007).

2 Margaret O'Hanlon, "Get Ready for Some Good News: HR Career Prospects Are Improving," *ERE Media*, January 24, 2013, accessed April 16, 2015, http://www.tlnt.com/2013/01/24/get-ready-for-some-good-news-hr-career-prospects-are-improving.

3 Alexander Hess, "10 Fastest-Growing Jobs in the USA," *USA Today*, September 2, 2013, accessed April 16, 2015, http://www.usatoday.com/story/money/business/2013/09/02/10-fastest-growing-jobs-in-usa/2750169.

4 Malcolm Gladwell, *Outliers: The Story of Success* (New York: Little, Brown, 2008). While Gladwell is most often cited for the ten-thousand-hour rule, the original citation is K. A. Ericsson, R. T. Krampe, and C. Tesch-Romer, "The Role of Deliberate Practice in the Acquisition of Expert Performance," *Psychological Review* 100 (1993): 393–94. Anders Ericsson says that it takes ten thousand hours (twenty hours for fifty weeks a year for ten years) of deliberate practice to become an expert in almost anything.

5 Thomas L. Friedman, *The World Is Flat: A Brief History of the Twenty-First Century* (New York: Farrar, Straus and Giroux, 2005).

6 Brent Conrad, "Media Statistics: Children's Use of TV, Internet, and Video Games," *TechAddiction*, http://www.techaddiction.ca/media-statistics.html.

7 L. von Ahn, "Turning Wasted Time on the Internet into Work" (paper presented at the Society for Human Resource

Management Thought Leaders Retreat, October 6, 2009, Scottsdale, Arizona).

8 "Top Twenty Businesses For 2015," *Small Business Opportunities*, October 6, 2014, accessed June 3, 2015, http://www.sbomag.com/2014/10/top-twenty-businesses.

CHAPTER 8

1 *The Wizard of Oz*, dir. Victor Flemming, Cukor George, and Vidor King, 1939.

CHAPTER 9

1 Sharon Perkins, "Most Common Genetic Diseases," *Livestrong.com*, February 18, 2014, accessed May 7, 2015, http://www.livestrong.com/article/253167-most-common-genetic-diseases.

2 Omar Khan, "Close Quarters and Bad Waters: The Perfect Storm for Disease Spread," *Penal Reform International*, November 6, 2013, accessed May 7, 2015, http://www.penalreform.org/blog/close-quarters-bad-waters-perfect-storm-disease-spread.

3 "Edmund Hillary Quotes," *BrainyQuote*, accessed May 10, 2015, http://www.brainyquote.com/quotes/authors/e/edmund_hillary.html.

CHAPTER 11

1 "Joe Montana Biography," *Encyclopedia of World Biography*, accessed May 7, 2015, http://www.notablebiographies.com/Mo-Ni/Montana-Joe.html.

2 Adam Augustyn, "Bo Jackson Biography—American Baseball and Football Player," *Encyclopedia Britannica*, accessed May 7, 2015, http://www.britannica.com/EBchecked/topic/1315317/Bo-Jackson.

CHAPTER 12

1 "Ed Diener," on the Pursuit of Happiness official website, accessed June 5, 2015, http://www.pursuit-of-happiness.org/history-of-happiness/ed-diener.

2 National Cancer Institute, "Increased Physical Activity Associated with Lower Risk of 13 Types of Cancer" (press release, May 16, 2016), http://www.cancer.gov/news-events/press-releases/2016/physical-activity-lowers-cancer-risk.

3 K. Weir, "The Exercise Effect," *Monitor on Psychology* 42, no. 11 (2011): 48.

4 D. Lee, R. Pate, C. Lavie, X. Sui, T. Church, and S. Blair, "Leisure-Time Running Reduces All-Cause and Cardiovascular Mortality Risk," *Journal of the American College of Cardiology* 64, no. 5 (2014): 472–81.

5 V. Lindlahr, *You Are What You Eat: How to Win and Keep Health with Diet* (1942; repr., Hollywood, CA: NewCastle, 1971).

6 "Steven Hawking Biography," *Biography.com*, http://www.biography.com/people/stephen-hawking-9331710#als-diagnosis.

7 Ben Evans, "Astronaut Don Thomas, Veteran of 'Repeat' Shuttle Mission, Turns 60 Today," *AmericaSpace*, May 6, 2015, accessed May 29, 2015, http://www.americaspace.com/?p=80877.

8 Dan Goleman, "Motivation: What Moves Us?," *Psychology Today*, December 28, 2011, accessed June 5, 2015, https://www.psychologytoday.com/blog/the-brain-and-emotional-intelligence/201112/motivation-what-moves-us.

CHAPTER 13

1 Douglas Rushkoff, "Are Jobs Obsolete?," *CNN*, September 7, 2011, http://www.cnn.com/2011/OPINION/09/07/rushkoff.jobs.obsolete.

2 Daniel Pink, *A Whole New Mind* (New York: Penguin Group, 2005).

3 Carmine Gallo, *The Presentation Secrets of Steve Jobs: How to Be Insanely Great in Front of Any Audience* (New York: McGraw-Hill, 2010).

4 Angela Lee Duckworth, "Angela Lee Duckworth: The Key to Success?," *TED: Ideas Worth Spreading*, April 2013, accessed June 5, 2015, http://www.ted.com/talks/angela_lee _duckworth_the_key_to_success_rit?language=en#t-354436.

5 J. Dutton, "Man of Steel," *Wired*, February 2013, 24.

6 Suicide Awareness Voices of Education, "Suicide Facts," *SAVE.org*, http://www.save.org/index.cfm?fuseaction =home.viewPage&page_id=705D5DF4-055B-F1EC -3F66462866FCB4E6.